Charley
LAU'S LAWS
ON HITTING

By Charley Lau Jr.
with Jeffrey Flanagan

Foreword by George Brett

ADDAX
PUBLISHING
GROUP

Published by Addax Publishing Group Inc.

Edited by An Beard

Designed by Randy Breeden

Cover Designed by Laura Bolter

For Information address:

Addax Publishing Group Inc.

8643 Hauser Drive, Suite 235, Lenexa, KS 66215

ISBN: 1-886110-95-6

Printed in the USA

1 3 5 7 9 10 8 6 4 2

ATTENTION SCHOOLS AND BUSINESSES

Addax Publishing Group Inc. books are available at quantity discounts
with bulk purchase for education, business, or sales promotional use.
For information, please write to:
Special Sales Department, Addax Publishing Group
8643 Hauser Drive, Suite 235, Lenexa, KS 66215

Library of Congress Cataloging-in-Publication Data

Lau, Charley.
    Lau's laws on hitting / by Charley Lau, Jr., with Jeffrey Flanagan ; foreword by George Brett.
    p. cm.
    ISBN 1-886110-95-6
    1. Batting (Baseball) I. Title: Laws on hitting. II. Flanagan, Jeffrey, 1959– III. Title.

GV869 .L385 2000
796.357'26—dc21   00-026941

What did the Lau System mean to me? After some experimentation and refinement, we came up with a stance and hitting approach for me that worked. And little did I realize at the time what it was going to do and how it was going to change my life. I've never looked back.

- George Brett, Hall of Famer and former Kansas City Royal

What this system taught me was how to think as a hitter. And that I think may be the most important part of hitting: knowing where the hits are, to right-center or left-center. It completely changed my approach to hitting.

- Hal McRae, former Royals great and hitting coach for the Philadelphia Phillies

The reason I stayed in the big leagues for 10 years was because of the Charley Lau Hitting System. He made me into a complete hitter. Charley Jr. has taken over the family business and truly enhanced the Lau Method of Hitting.

- Vance Law, former major leaguer and
  head baseball coach at Brigham Young University

The other hitting books out on the market are only generic attempts at fixing the baseball swing. You shouldn't put a Band-Aid on your swing, you need to fix it. Charley Lau Jr.'s system is the only one that will fix your swing.

- Jesse Barfield, 1986 American League Home Run Champion

Dedication

This book is dedicated to my father and the gift that he gave us all. Thank you and God bless you, Dad. Thank you for what you've given me.

Also, to Lisa, who with her patience and caring helped me in many ways. She has helped me achieve many goals. Without you, this book wouldn't have been possible.

– Charley Lau Jr.

I'd like to dedicate this to my Uncle Kenny, who passed away during the writing of the book. A Brewers fan, a Packers fan, you will be missed.

– Jeffrey Flanagan

Acknowledgments

As the son of a major league hitting instructor, I grew up without a father physically around me. That doesn't mean he didn't have a profound effect on my life. But his absence made me grow nearer to another pivotal figure in my life – Dan Yeary, a pastor and a very dear friend. He helped shape my character and was always there for me. I can't imagine my life without his presence. I'd also like to thank George Brett for his class, or perhaps I should call it his Hall of Fame class. Without George, my father's teachings may never have garnered the respect they do today.

I'd like to thank my co-author, Jeffrey Flanagan. He did a great job. Jeffrey brought my thoughts out, and it wasn't very difficult for me to communicate with him because he's a very intelligent baseball guy. So actually, it was a lot of fun doing the project with him. I'd like to thank Addax Publishing, too, for realizing the potential that this book had and for taking a chance and making this possible. I want to thank all those major league hitters who let their top hand fly off the bat and hit all those home runs and have such high batting averages. I don't have to list their names because all you have to do is look at the lists of the game's top hitters. They're there. Those guys are keeping Lau's Laws very much alive in baseball.

A special thank you to Kazuma Sports, Markwort Sporting Goods and my good friends Jeff Cross, Charley Nobles and Don Smiley for their support.

– Charley Lau Jr.

There are so many people to thank, starting with Charley Lau Jr., who trusted me with the words that communicated his message. Charley, if only I'd had you as an instructor when I was growing up, I might have been what I always dreamed of being – a professional baseball player. I'd also like to thank all the people who had to listen to me gripe about the work that went into this project, starting with my mom, Luanne Grignon, who always was there with support. I need to thank my mentor, Steve Cameron, who saved my career as a writer and restored my faith in the written word. And I'd like to thank some of my pals for their pats on my shoulder during the many hours of writing – Barry Holmes, Craig Glazer and Natalie Brown. Thank you all.

–Jeffrey Flanagan

Table of contents

Foreword by George Brett

Some people think that I could have been the player I was and made it to the Hall of Fame without having met Charley Lau and without using his system of hitting. Well, there's absolutely no way I could have become the player I was without Charley. I never even hit .300 in the minors. And in 1974, when Charley was the batting coach for the Royals, he came up, put his arm around me and said, "George, I want to challenge you to become a better hitter. Are you ready and willing to try?" I was hitting about .200 at the time with about 200 at-bats. We threw out everything I'd been taught about hitting and started working on his techniques – releasing the top hand, loading up your weight on your back side, exploding through the ball and the biggest thing, extending your lead arm through the swing. From then on, my average kept climbing. We kept setting goals, like hitting .250 by this time and .270 by that time, and I kept surpassing those goals and we had to set new goals. Charley and his system changed my life. And he also became as close to me as anyone, like a second dad.

I knew Charley Jr. from the time he was a little kid. And he has taken his father's system and expanded it. Trust me, this is the only system you will ever need to know in order to hit a baseball. Charley Jr. knows what he's talking about and through this book you will learn the best way to hit. It's no secret why guys like Mark McGwire went from hitting 40 homers a year to 60 or 70: It's the lead-arm extension. I see it everywhere in baseball now. I see everyone using the Lau System of hitting. Try this system of hitting and you will never regret it.

–George Brett, Hall of Famer, former Kansas City Royal

Preface

Like many young boys, I learned the art of hitting a baseball from my father. But the difference between other boys and myself was that my dad was Charley Lau, the most influential and famous hitting coach in the history of the game. As sons sometimes do, though, I questioned my father's methods. And I was not alone. Despite his extraordinary and unparalleled success, my father's theories on hitting were first met with skepticism and ridicule. Indeed, my father's teachings were considered radical at the time because they challenged the very core of baseball's old school hitting philosophies. But in the face of that criticism my father persevered, and his success with his students eventually made a believer out of me. I wanted to learn more, and quickly became a passionate student of hitting.

Then, when I was 18, I lost my father to cancer. I was on my own, alone, without the mentor who could answer my questions. But even in his absence, I became obsessed with his theories on hitting. I studied. I researched. I began analyzing each method's effectiveness by scrutinizing all types of hitters, video-by-video, frame-by-frame, and catalogued the strengths and weaknesses of their approaches. In the end, as many sons do, I found out that father knows best.

Today, as it was when I was a boy, most hitters learn how to hit based on information passed on from previous generations. Unfortunately, much of this information is misguided and serves only to handicap players at all levels. As a result, sadly, most hitters never develop their full potential. So why don't more hitters and hitting instructors question this outdated information? Are they afraid to challenge the theories of baseball's old school? Or do they feel that hitting education may, in fact, constrain a hitter's natural ability? Perhaps the answer is yes on both counts because this much is unmistakable: Ignorance about hitting is rampant in today's game at all levels. I have witnessed countless hitters, close up and from afar, who continue to struggle despite their obvious physical talents. Further contributing to the problem is the lack of teaching today, either because hitting coaches are not equipped themselves to properly instruct or are rendered powerless by employers unwilling to acknowledge new philosophies. With the tools and technology available today, this is unacceptable.

As a student of hitting and a hitting coach, I personally believe that today's baseball player can never know too much about the art of hitting. It is through education that a hitter can understand what his body must do to effectively hit a baseball. With the application of that knowledge through practice, his performance can improve dramatically. The more time the hitter spends drilling his mind and body together in the proper mechanics, the more prepared he becomes in game situations. As with any motor skills movement, the act of hitting a baseball needs to be consciously learned, then subconsciously performed. This assures spontaneous reaction.

As I have suggested, the blind acceptance of information passed on from previous generations is the primary reason that the evolution of hitting has been stalled. Incredibly, many of today's debates on hitting are the same as they were over 30 years ago, such as the controversies over hip rotation versus weight shift, and the top-versus-bottom-hand dominance. The misunderstanding of these topics continues to hamper the pure and successful teaching of hitting.

The debate over top-versus-bottom-hand dominance led my father to experiment with the release of the top hand after contact. He believed this technique improved the swing dramatically by allowing it to continue on its arc. Furthermore, he believed that a level plane of the hands as they extend through the ball allowed for the ball to carry further. These findings were not accepted by many baseball purists at that time and are still heatedly argued aspects of successful hitting development today.

In my quest to resolve these debates and achieve my goal of becoming the most effective hitting instructor possible, I must confess I struggled with these issues myself. My father's research gave me a starting point and a solid foundation. Thus, I have spent the past 10 years studying the best hitters, past and present, and have discovered their common denominators. I also have applied the laws of physics, motion, biomechanics and kinesiology to formulate a hitting system that allows hitters to maximize their talents. Through this relentless study of the swing, I have been able to thoroughly resolve these debates on hitting for myself and my students. Many of the elite hitters of today incorporate what we call Lau's Laws in their hitting approaches. Despite the obvious success of these hitters, others in baseball continue to blindly accept the old school beliefs.

This brings us to the purpose of this book: to educate hitters, coaches, mothers and fathers by providing them practical instruction on how to apply this knowledge. This book contains the benefits of my father's and my own lifelong studies on the art of hitting. I identify the mistruths, dispel the myths, and most importantly, unveil the most comprehensive swing development program available. This program includes specific drills and exercises, personal practice programs and the most effective mental approach to hitting. I guarantee your improvement by teaching you how to deliver maximum force with the most energy-efficient swing on a consistent basis.

This book is intended for hitters at all levels, from little leaguers to major leaguers, and to those who coach them. After reading this book, you will have a clear understanding of what happens during the most successful swings, and how to handle pitches in all locations of the strike zone. You will learn how to practice and make adjustments to eliminate your weaknesses. Not only will you have the proof of your own success, but you will be able to validate that success by observing the greatest hitters in baseball today display these secrets as well. Until now, you have probably been misled and handicapped by what you have been told about hitting. Giving you the knowledge you need to perform and/or teach the art of hitting is the inspiration behind my writing this book. Yes, it's time to finally lay to rest all the outdated notions of past generations about hitting.

We begin with an overview of hitting today and how we arrived here. I review the most popular hitting philosophies and evaluate the advantages and disadvantages of each. This book will give readers the information they need to choose the best philosophy to improve their own hitting. I reveal my own secret formula for developing the most dynamic swing possible using a step-by-step approach.

I constantly strive to improve myself as a teacher and as a student of hitting. With my father's philosophy and the system I have developed as my own contribution to the art of hitting, you will benefit through quick and unparalleled success. I challenge little leaguers, big leaguers, mothers, fathers and coaches everywhere to try this step-by-step system. I get results because I look beyond the obvious and conventional. I study, challenge and experiment. Perhaps that is the most important lesson I ever learned from my father, Charley Lau Sr. And I'll end this introduction with the single most important piece of advice my father ever gave me:

"Believe with your eyes, not with your ears!"

Charley Lau Jr.

Chapter 1:

The Revolution and Evolution of Hitting

Over the last 10 years there has been nothing short of a revolution in hitting. The result has been an unparalleled improvement in the productivity of the hitter. In this chapter, I will discuss the evolution of hitting, focusing on the present revolution and its impact on the technique and effectiveness of today's hitters. I also will talk about some of the theories and technologies that have advanced hitting to its present state.

A Pinnacle Time

Countless theories have been proposed to explain the absolutely staggering offensive explosion in Major League Baseball in recent years. By far the most popular of them has been the juiced-ball theory. Still, others point to expansion and the subsequent diluting of pitching talent, or the wave of new, smaller ballparks. Some even suggest that hitters simply are bigger and stronger. Yet, none of these theories offers a comprehensive explanation.

Very few people, it seems, consider another alternative: That today's hitters have improved their technique and their approach to hitting. During recent seasons, and particularly the 1996 season, I watched and analyzed swings. What I concluded was that today's hitters are demonstrating technique better than any of their predecessors.

The Juiced-Ball Theory

Every time there is a deluge of home runs in Major League Baseball, you're bound to hear cries of "Juiced ball!" The juiced-ball theory contends that the baseball is wound tighter, thus it is harder and more likely to travel further. Given that the home run remains the most marketable occurrence in baseball, and that the game's higher-ups are trying to lure fans back, one can easily see why the juiced-ball theory garners so much support. Yet for all the hitters that had a career high in home runs in 1996, there were many other bona fide home run hitters who didn't match or beat their career best. For example, Fred McGriff, one of the most prolific home run hitters of our time, fell off to just 28 homers in 1996. Albert Belle, who hit 50 in the 1994 abbreviated season, dropped to 48 in 1996.

The Expansion Theory

Many baseball purists blame expansion, claiming it has decreased the quality of pitching, and therefore increased offensive production. This watered-down pitching theory, to some degree, may be plausible, though by the same argument you would have to concede that the hitter's pool also would be diluted. Clearly, it isn't. And what also is overlooked in this argument is the growing number of countries from which baseball now scouts for its pitching pool. Baseball has expanded far beyond United States borders, and pitching talent is imported from Japan, Puerto Rico, Venezuela, the Dominican Republic, Nicaragua, Australia, Korea and Cuba. The lure of big money in American baseball is more than enough incentive to attract the finest baseball players from all over the globe. Without question, the talent pool from which to choose from is at an all-time high.

There also has been a big change in the last 20 years in the way pitchers are utilized. Instead of seeing the same pitcher for eight or more innings, hitters now sometimes face four, five or even six pitchers a game. And with each new pitcher a hitter must adjust and adapt to a new repetoire of pitches. A new delivery. A new release point. New speed. As a result, today's hitter is in a constant mode of adjustment, from one at-bat to the next, and with that comes the increased probability of failure.

The Smaller Ballparks Theory

Of all the theories, the smaller ballpark theory holds the most validity. Today's rash of new ballparks indeed are smaller and more hitter friendly. Brady Anderson represents a prime example. After adjusting to the cozy dimensions of Camden Yards, Anderson went from 20 home runs in 1995 to 50 in 1996. Anderson's sudden long-ball ability was eye-popping. But remember this: Anderson hit over half his home runs that year on the road.

The Bigger, Stronger Hitters Theory

It is impossible to dispute the fact that today's hitters are bigger, stronger and in better shape. Most players spend their off-season laboring in the weight room, and virtually every organization today employs a full-time strength and conditioning coach. But there is always a flip side. Pitchers, too, have the same equipment and conditioning technology available to them. Same goes for fielders, who are faster, more athletic and capable of far better defense than their predecessors.

The Good Technique Theory

So if all these theories don't fully explain the hitting revolution, what does? In one word: technique. It is clear to me that hitters today have improved greatly in their approach and their technique. And that fact, more than anything, explains the rise in offensive production and the runaway inflation of earned run averages.

High batting averages and power to all fields is what the best hitters possess today. The reason for their success often is misunderstood and, therefore, difficult to imitate. By analyzing the top hitters in baseball today, I will show you that they overwhelmingly subscribe to a specific philosophy, one that displays the most effective mechanics for a swing and thus reveals the secrets to success for the next generation of hitters.

A Question of Mechanics

When it comes to the mechanics of a baseball swing, the questions are endless. Should you swing up or down? Do the hips rotate? Is there a weight transfer? How does one create bat speed? What kind of stance is the most effective? Can the ball be hit farther if you pull it or use the whole field? Is the bottom hand or top hand the source of power? Does taking the top hand off the bat after contact diminish power?

If you hit off the front foot, do you lessen your power? To answer these questions, we must test the accuracy of the two most prominent philosophies of hitting.

The Start of a Revolution

The art of hitting has never been stagnant. It has evolved with each generation of hitters, who make incremental improvements in technique. Over the past 10 years, however, the changes have been more revolutionary than evolutionary. The game is developing a new generation of hitting stars who are more complete and more potent than any in the game's history. Not only do they maintain high batting averages, they also are a threat to hit to all fields with exceptional power. Having eliminated many of the philosophical weaknesses of their predecessors, this new generation patrols the entire strike zone. As a result, pitchers have begun to respond to this challenge with a change in their approach and philosophy.

To fully appreciate this hitting revolution and its impact on the game, it is vital to understand the most influential hitting philosophies and how they have affected today's hitter. I will compare the two predominant hitting influences in baseball history, the Ted Williams Rotational System and the late Charley Lau's Weight Shift and Extension System.

The Ted Williams Philosophy

Ted Williams' Rotational System stemmed from his own success as a pull hitter.

In the Ted Williams era there was no technology available to validate his rotational system of hitting. Naturally, many people accepted his philosophy because of his tremendous personal success.

Most of the power hitters from that era attempted to pull virtually every pitch based on the belief that one could hit the ball farther down the left- or right-field line than one could to any other part of the field. Of course, the best pitch to pull is one thrown on the inner half of the plate. But because contact then has to be made farther out in front of the plate, the hitter becomes vulnerable. Off-speed pitches and balls thrown on the outer half of the plate make a pull hitter's hips open too soon, taking him out of the hitting area. Due to this premature opening of the hips, pull hitters become one-dimensional and susceptible to strikeouts and routine groundouts. Even the best pull hitters have an extremely high strikeout ratio and usually manage little more than a .260 batting average. Smart pitchers pitch this type of hitter on the outside part of the plate, which exposes the hitter's all-or-nothing approach.

Through the years, pitchers took advantage of the pull hitter's vulnerability. The flaws in this system therefore became more apparent. Still, who had the nerve to question the philosophy of the one and only Ted Williams? My father, Charley Lau, did. And you can imagine the immediate reaction from baseball's old-school disciples when my father, a lifetime .256 hitter, challenged the hitting philosophy of the great Ted Williams.

The Charley Lau Philosophy

My father had been a journeyman catcher and was not blessed with Cooperstown ability. An elbow injury ended his playing career in 1967 and in that same year he became the Baltimore Orioles hitting instructor. His first assignment was to improve the young and slick fielding shortstop who had never hit his weight in the major leagues. That shortstop's name was Mark Belanger. By the end of the 1969 season, Belanger, under the guidance of my father's teachings, hit an amazing (for him) .287, a full 80 points higher than he had hit in any previous season.

But after my father's request of a $1,000 raise was denied by the O's, he moved on to the Oakland A's and his next projects: Joe Rudi and Dave Duncan.

Clearly, my father was onto something big. He was establishing an impressive list of successful students who had adhered to his teaching philosophies. All that was lacking was indisputable proof to justify his assault on the old school beliefs of hitting. For this, my father needed an environment conducive to learning and experimentation. Enter the Kansas City Royals, a team still in its expansion infancy, and a team willing to explore new concepts. And so the memorable marriage between the Royals and my father, and a new dawn of hitting instruction, began.

Chapter Two:

The VCR:
Changing Baseball Forever

By the 1970s, technology had undergone its own revolution. And by far the most significant advancement in technology, in Charley Lau's mind, was the invention of the video cassette recorder. The VCR. With this new tool, my father was able to slow a swing down frame-by-frame, analyze it, and thereby unlock the secrets of successful hitting. My father literally lived with this machine. And, as a young boy, I witnessed many of his ground-breaking discoveries. My father began by studying footage of the greatest hitters of all time, from Ruth to Gehrig to Musial to Mays. And yes, even the great Ted Williams. My father was astounded. He was convinced that hitting had been poorly taught throughout the years, and that misguided information had been passed on blindly from coach to player and from generation to generation without the slightest regard for analytical study or questioning.

Because the home run always has captured our curiosity, my father studied tape of the most prolific home run hitter of all time, Hank Aaron. In the Aaron era, baseball's hitting instructors still believed that hitters should keep their weight on their back foot as they swung, instead of transferring their weight to their front leg during the swing. This method supposedly would prevent a hitter from lunging forward with the upper body and subsequently losing the powerful rotation of the hip. Hitting against your front leg and turning on the back ball of the foot was, according to this philosophy, the only deterrent to the uncontrolled lunge.

But my father was highly suspicious of this doctrine and also believed that many of the game's best hitters at the time ignored the back-foot theory. And my father's eyes confirmed his beliefs when he viewed a tape of Aaron's swing. Not only was Aaron not on his back foot, but his swing was so powerful that his back foot was *off the ground* at the point of contact. Imagine this. Here was undeniable evidence that the most prolific hitter of all time was a front-foot hitter.

With this revelation, my dad began examining tape of the most successful sluggers of all time. He uncovered some amazing similarities. As did Aaron, a majority of these hitters were transferring their weight to, not against, their front leg. At the point of impact, their back toe was pointing toward the pitcher's mound and their back heel towards the sky. They were not staying on the ball of their back foot, which had been known as "squishing the bug."

Furthermore, my father noticed that while hitters had unique styles, the most successful hitters all arrived at the same power positions in a timely manner and did so in a specific sequence. My father concluded that this sequence represented the most biomechanically sound utilization of the hitter's body and resulted in the most energy-efficient swing possible.

These discoveries were major breakthroughs. The back-foot hitter who had been taught to hit against his front leg could pull the ball, but he had difficulty hitting the ball to the gap and over to the opposite foul line. My father believed this fact made the back-foot hitter an incomplete hitter. Conversely, the front-foot hitter could drive the ball to all fields. This ability to hit to all fields, despite the pitch location, represented a powerful defense against pitchers.

The Absolutes of Hitting

My father used these breakthroughs to formulate his legendary Absolutes of Hitting. These Absolutes were essential in understanding and communicating the teaching of the swing. While hitters possessed different stances and held their bats in different places, they all shared one common denominator: They all arrived in one specific position in order to swing in the most biomechanically effective way. This was the essence of the Absolutes. The Absolutes are not a crazed theory, but instead a proven way of teaching and understanding what is necessary to effectively use your body during the swing. This was the premise that my father used to become the best hitting instructor in baseball history.

You may wonder how Charley Lau became such a great hitting instructor when his own performance as a hitter was less than stellar. The fact is that hitting and teaching hitting are hardly one in the same. History has shown that in any sport, very few of the great athletes become great coaches or instructors. No, what makes a sound instructor often is the determination to study the subject as an art. Many of the great athletes through time would be hard-pressed to actually convey how they became great. Sometimes, quite often actually, it requires someone more familiar with failure to be able to teach someone else how to succeed.

Knowledge is King

Never underestimate the value of knowledge. Sure, some athletes are simply blessed with natural ability and seem to require little mentoring at all. Hey, but not everyone is Michael Jordan. The rest of us need teaching. Consider, for a minute, the concept of motor memory. Whatever your body does consistently becomes a habit. You were taught to tie your shoes a certain way. Your parents showed you how, step by step, and you practiced over and over again. After awhile, you were able to tie your shoes with your eyes closed. Now, imagine how much longer it would have taken you to learn if you hadn't had a parent show you the mechanics. True, through trial and error, you eventually would have figured it out. But perhaps not as efficiently and certainly not as quickly. The same principle is true in hitting a baseball, which many experts consider the most difficult feat in sports. While talent can go far, learning the Absolutes from a knowledgeable instructor will get you there quicker.

My point is you need the proper mental nourishment to feed your physical body. If you don't understand the physics of the swing, you cannot train your body successfully to perform that swing. Furthermore, to maintain any level of success you must first understand what makes you successful.

My father believed that by simply having proper mechanics you consistently would make contact and, perhaps, hit more home runs. Since body type and strength differs from player to player, he also believed that everyone should utilize their best attributes. In other words, if you are small and not very strong, you shouldn't strive to be a home run hitter. Instead, make your goal to hit the ball hard wherever it is pitched.

Pull, Don't Push

The most controversial aspect in the evolution of hitting has been the path and follow-through of the swing. For decades, hitting instructors had taught hitters to push the swing through the hitting zone with their top hand. Then, much like a forehand in the tennis swing, the hitter was supposed to roll over his hands after contact to finish the follow-through. My father wrestled with this notion and believed it to be as incorrect as the back-foot theory. Extension was so vitally important in the proper throwing of the baseball that my father believed the same principle applied to the swing. Just as in throwing a baseball, if you don't have the proper extension in the swing, the baseball would not carry for distance. Also, if you were to dominate with your top hand you would impart a topspin and cut your swing off prematurely, retarding the swing. Backspin was what my father believed to be essential in driving the baseball consistently.

My father also believed that hitters had difficulty extending through the swing with two hands. So he began experimenting with players by having them take the top hand off the bat after contact before the top hand rolled over and cut off the swing. After the top hand came off, the lead arm or bottom hand, by nature, had to keep going until it became completely extended. Only then did it roll over and finish the swing. This action of the hands allowed the bat to stay flat through the hitting zone longer, thus covering the whole area of the strike zone for a longer time, and also allowed more acceleration in the swing. The follow-through produced backspin instead of topspin, allowing the ball to carry farther. It also allowed the hitter to transfer the body's weight more aggressively, translating into more power. This was radical thinking at the time and some non-believers still criticize it to this day. But as we will see later, this approach has been adopted by the greatest hitters today and is the vehicle to successful hitting.

Be Wary of Bad Advice

Most of us know baseball from what we were taught by our coaches in Little League, high school, and if we survived, college. We listen intently, and automatically assume that these instructors are well-informed. But how many of these instructors have ever truly studied hitting or independently confirmed their teachings? Unfortunately, very few. And, in fact, it has been my experience that the majority of instructors, even at the professional level, are grossly uninformed. For example, if you took a poll of every professional hitting instructor on what he believed was essential to building a successful swing, you would get far too many different answers to draw any conclusion. And most of these coaches have devoted their lives to baseball.

To truly understand how to teach hitting, you must become a student of the art. I, personally, have used video tape to verify the truths and validity of my father's Absolutes and I fully appreciate their significance. Studying the swing is critical. As you know, the swing unfolds so fast that it's impossible to break down with the naked eye at regular speed. Try it yourself. Tape a swing and watch it at regular speed. Then slow it down frame-by-frame. This is the only way to understand the mechanics of the swing. This is how I have catalogued all the hitters who take the top hand off the bat. I also use slow motion video to detect the flaws in swings and use that as a teaching tool for my students. Never be afraid to question. Keep asking yourself: Where am I getting my knowledge of hitting from? Is the person instructing me equipped with the necessary information? For openers, compare the instruction you're getting with the following.

Charley Lau Sr.'s Absolutes of Hitting
Taken from *The Art of Hitting .300* (1980)

- A balanced, workable stance.

- Rhythm and movement that will maintain that balance.

- Striding with the front toe closed.

- A good weight shift from the back leg to the front leg.

- Having the bat in the launch position when the stride is completed.

- An aggressive move towards the pitcher when swinging.

- A tension-free swing.

- Keeping your head down at the point of contact.

- Using the whole field to hit in.

- Hitting through the ball with a good finish of the swing.

With the use of slow-motion video, my father possessed an essential tool to learning. With this tool he was able to develop a formula for success. No one else in baseball history had studied the swing this way before, simply because the technology didn't exist.

Lau's Accomplishments

My father had the ideal situation when he started working for the expansion Kansas City Royals. It was a young and eager organization filled with young and eager players trying to make a dent in Oakland's dominance of the American League

West. The Royals were, and here's the key, receptive to new ideas. Kansas City also played in a new ballpark at the time, carpeted by Astroturf, a fact that steered the hierarchy away from slow-footed power hitters and more toward doubles and triples hitters. The Royals had some decent young talent, such as George Brett, a third baseman who had never hit .300 in the minor leagues, but who flashed potential. They also had an outfielder named Hal McRae, a fiery player who had yet to develop the discipline at the plate to be a consistent performer.

Being a hitting instructor requires more than knowledge. You need the ability to communicate to each individual player in a separate fashion that they'll understand. My father targeted the less successful players first. He scheduled early hitting practice every day with a few willing pupils, patiently making suggestions and using his video machine to illustrate his points. It wasn't long before my father's message started to sink in.

Quite often the most successful players resist instruction, and, especially, new ideas. It often takes a severe dose of failure before a player admits he needs help. Hal McRae was a clear example. His glaring failure early on with the Royals prompted a session with my father. Success soon followed and McRae and the rest of the Royals began to believe in my father's teachings. Putting the ball in play and manufacturing runs became the Royals' signature style of offense. George Brett's batting average was at .220 when Dad approached the young rookie and said, "You're not going to have success with that approach." Under Dad's wing, Brett transformed himself and his swing and became one of the most feared hitters in baseball.

In 1976, the Lau impact clearly became evident. Kansas City had challenged the Oakland A's for the Western Division title. Two of his students, Brett and McRae, were competing for the batting title on the last day of the season. Brett won the batting title .333 to McRae's .332, and Kansas City wound up in the playoffs ahead of the favored Oakland A's.

My father finally started getting his due for transforming some no-names into pennant contenders. Virtually every player adhered to the Lau Absolutes, most notably taking the top hand off the bat to improve the follow-through on their swings.

In 1977, the Royals won 102 games and my father could claim another success story. He turned Al Cowens into a slugger. Cowens had hit .265 with three home runs in 1976. But under the tutelage of my father, Cowens hit .312 with 23 home runs and 112 RBIs in 1977. As a team the Royals went from 65 home runs in 1976 to 146 home runs in 1977, despite playing in a homer-unfriendly ballpark. And still, in both seasons, the team led the league in doubles, triples and runs scored.

Divorce from the Royals

With free-agency running rampant, the richer teams flexed their financial muscle and scooped up the top players. Kansas City, however, used a different approach. It relied on player development and on solid instruction from people like my father.

But in 1978, his contract was up with the Royals and it was no secret that then-manager Whitey Herzog was jealous that a hitting coach was getting most of the credit for the Royals' rise to perennial contender. It was clear he would never work with the Royals again, at least as long as Herzog was the manager. This bothered my father. We were so close to all the Royals players that we felt like a big family. I had spent so many summers with those guys and I idolized Brett. And like any Royals fan, I also hated the Yankees because they ended our playoff run three years in a row.

During that off-season my father began looking for a new team. And of all teams to sign with, where did my dad find employment? You guessed it. I still remember the headline: "Yankees Sign Lau to Multi-Year Contract." The best team that money could buy had just bought the best hitting instructor.

No Power Outage in Lau System

It has often been said that the Ted Williams method of hitting is better for power hitters and that the Charley Lau method provides a higher batting average while sacrificing power. Baloney. Under my father's teachings, team home runs by the Royals increased dramatically. And the Yankees went from 125 home runs in 1978 (pre-Lau) to 150 in 1979 with my father as batting coach. In 1980, the Yankees hit 189 homers. Even Reggie Jackson, not the most likely candidate to listen to a hitting instructor, took advice from my father. And he was greatly rewarded, increasing his home run total from 27 in 1979 to a league-leading 41 in 1980. Jackson also hit .300 for the first and only time in his career. It was no coincidence that Jackson began taking his top hand off the bat in batting practice to improve his follow-through, He finished second in the American League Most-Valuable Player race that year (unfortunately for him, Brett hit .390 that season, the highest average since Ted Williams' .406). Brett, youll recall, won the MVP and his second batting title in 1980. The Royals also beat the Yankees for the first time in the playoffs, led by Brett's dramatic home run in the upper deck at Yankee Stadium off Goose Gossage in the decisive game.

As NBC's Bob Costas interviewed Brett while reviewing a replay of the three-run homer, Costas gushed, "That's the nicest swing in baseball." And Brett's response? "God bless you, Charley Lau. Without you, I would have been a construction worker." Brett always gave my father the credit for his success, even pointing to the sky, teary-eyed, and thanking my father during his Hall of Fame speech in the summer of 1999. Without question, Brett was the poster boy of my father's teachings right down to the patented top-hand release during the follow-through of the swing. Brett became the most feared hitter in baseball and is the only player in history to win three batting titles in three different decades. He hit .333 in 1976, .390 in 1980 and .335 in 1990.

In 1981, the Yankees and my father worked their way back to the World Series before losing to the Dodgers. In my father's three-year tenure with the Yankees, they had significantly increased in all offensive categories. When his contract was up in New York, he already had become a household name in the world of hitting. And he had a best selling book out called: *The Art of Hitting .300*. In short, he had his choice of teams. He took his time before making a decision.

The Legacy Left Behind

My father finally made his decision by signing a six-year contract (a record for a hitting coach) before the 1982 season with the Tony LaRussa-managed Chicago White Sox, who hadn't been in the playoffs since 1959. My father's first objective was to transform White Sox catcher Carlton Fisk into a power hitter in spacious Comiskey Park. You know the rest. Fisk wound up hitting more home runs (376) than any catcher in baseball history. The secret of his success? Top-hand release, as instructed by my father. As a team, the White Sox increased their home runs from 76 to 136 upon the arrival of their new hitting coach.

In 1983, the White Sox began scoring runs in record amounts and after one year under my father's instruction, they won a division crown by scoring over 800 runs, tops in the majors. Along the way, another success story emerged. Vance Law, a rather run-of-the-mill hitter, increased his home run total from three to 17 in one year, and contributed significantly to the team's success.

But sadly, that year it became apparent that my father was having health problems. Soon after, he was diagnosed with cancer. Even then, he continued to coach his hitters from his hospital bed. He spoke with hitters over the phone and reviewed video tapes from his room. He died the next spring, on March 18, 1984.

My father's courageous assault on the old school beliefs produced more than just isolated cases of success. In fact, he originated a whole new understanding of hitting. And his legacy lives on today. You want evidence? Examine the following charts, which identify the hitters in today's game who still adhere to the Lau Absolutes, from releasing the top hand during the follow-through to front-foot hitting.

For the sake of argument, let's examine the season of 1996, considered the breakthrough season for today's offensive dominance.

1996 Major League Home Run Leaders
American and National League Combined

Hitter	1996 Team	HRs	Top Hand Front-foot hitter	Release
Mark McGwire	Oakland	52	N	Y
Brady Anderson	Baltimore	50	Y	Y
Ken Griffey	Seattle	49	Y	Y
Albert Belle	Cleveland	48	Y	Y
Andres Galarraga	Colorado	47	Y	Y
Juan Gonzalez	Texas	47	Y	Y
Jay Buhner	Seattle	44	Y	Y
Mo Vaughn	Boston	44	Y	N
Barry Bonds	San Francisco	42	N	Y
Gary Sheffield	Florida	42	Y	Y
Todd Hundley	N.Y. Mets	41	Y	Y
Ken Caminiti	San Diego	40	Y	Y

Numbers don't lie. Eleven out of the top 12 home run hitters took their top hand off the bat. Obviously, taking your top hand off the bat doesn't diminish power.

Now let's look at batting averages and slugging percentages of the top hitters from 1997-1999 and see which ones have top-hand release and which ones are front-foot hitters.

1997 American League

Player	Batting Average	Front-foot hitter	Top-hand release
Frank Thomas	.347	Y	Y
Edgar Martinez	.330	Y	Y
David Justice	.329	Y	Y
Bernie Williams	.328	Y	Y
Manny Ramirez	.328	Y	Y

1997 National League

Player	Batting Average	Front-foot hitter	Top-hand release
Tony Gwynn	.372	Y	Y
Larry Walker	.366	Y	Y
Mike Piazza	.362	Y	N
Kenny Lofton	.333	Y	Y
Wally Joyner	.327	Y	Y

1997 American League

Player	Slugging Percentage	Front-foot hitter	Top-hand release
Ken Griffey Jr.	.646	Y	Y
Frank Thomas	.611	Y	Y
David Justice	.596	Y	Y
Juan Gonzalez	.589	Y	Y
Jim Thome	.579	N	N

1997 National League

Player	Slugging Percentage	Front-foot hitter	Top-hand release
Larry Walker	.720	Y	Y
Mike Piazza	.638	Y	N
Jeff Bagwell	.592	N	N
Andres Galarraga	.585	Y	Y
Ray Lankford	.585	Y	N

Or let's look at the famous 1998 National League home run race:

Player	HRs	Front-foot hitter	Top-hand release
Mark McGwire	70	N	Y
Sammy Sosa	66	Y	Y
Greg Vaughn	50	N	Y
Vinny Castilla	46	Y	N
Andres Galarraga	44	Y	Y

And the 1999 American League home run race

Ken Griffey Jr.	48	Y	Y
Rafael Palmeiro	47	Y	Y
Carlos Delgado	44	Y	N
Manny Ramirez	44	Y	Y
Shawn Green	42	Y	Y
Alex Rodriguez	42	Y	Y

And finally, the 1999 National League batting-title race

Player	Batting Average	Front-foot hitter	Top-hand release
Larry Walker	.379	Y	Y
Luis Gonzalez	.336	Y	Y
Bobby Abreu	.335	Y	N
Sean Casey	.332	Y	N
Jeff Cirillo	.326	Y	N

Chapter 3:

The Stance, Swing Preparation and Stride

Hitting, like any other athletic endeavor, involves a combination of fundamentals (elements one finds in any successful athletic movement) and preferences (choices one makes to achieve the desired results). Fundamentals involve the elements of a motion necessary to utilize the body for maximum results. Preferences are the choices one makes to be the hitter he wants to be, and the things he needs to do to adhere to the laws of physics and motion.

Every hitter is unique in what they do to hit a baseball. We have seen successful hitters use high hands in their stance such as Hall of Famer Carl Yastrzemski. We have seen batting champions hit from an open stance and stride toward the pitcher, hitters such as Andres Galarraga. We have seen batting champions such as Rogers Hornsby and Keith Hernandez hit from a closed stance. We have seen successful hitters such as Pete Rose and Jeff Bagwell hit from a deep crouch. We have seen back-foot hitters such as Mark McGwire and front-foot hitters such as Frank Thomas. We have seen the no-stride swings of Joe DiMaggio, Jose Canseco and Paul Molitor. And we have seen the high-leg kicks from Juan Gonzalez, Manny Ramirez and Kirby Puckett.

Each of these types of hitters has elements unique to their hitting style (preferences) and each possesses elements that are universal (fundamentals). All of these hitters are unique and each one of them is a great hitter. Let me explain. Hitters have had different stances for years and will continue to do so forever. But we often fail to notice is that they all arrive at the same powerful position the body needs in order to produce and execute the most effective swing. In other words, hitters have different styles but must use the same technique to properly tap into the dynamics and power of their individual bodies.

All we need do is look to science in order to define the proper approach to hitting mechanics. The problem arises when we look at a particular player and his so-called fundamentals. In reality, these so-called funadamentals are really only preferences the individual needed for them to hit. The result is a great model for the individual but too often a flawed model for anyone else trying to imitate. So let's examine fundamentals and determine just how something becomes a fundamental or, as we'll call them, Lau's Laws.

A fundamental must adhere to three criteria: first, it must be something that a majority of all successful hitters do the same; second, it must adhere to how the human body is designed to function most dynamically and efficiently; and third, it must adhere to the laws of physics and motion.

What Are the Fundamentals?

- Level eyes – for tracking and for connecting hand-eye coordination, and for balance.

- Balance – achieved by the proper posture in the stance.

- Acceleration of energy – utilizing the body's motion.

- Proper sequence – the most efficient transfer of that acceleration of energy.

In any sport, success derives from a consistent alignment of the body that enables the athlete to deliver his maximum force with as little wasted movement as possible. This is especially true for the baseball swing. The problem in analyzing the best body alignment is that the swing happens too fast for our eyes to register the movement. We often miss the biomechanical similarities of the best hitters. But understand this: All hitters utilize the same vehicle or position to deliver their devastating blows to a baseball. And there is only one position that body eventually reaches in delivering maximum force. All great hitters eventually get to this position.

Let's start with the way we hold the bat — the grip. Our hands are the only part of the body that touches the bat, so it is important that we hold the bat properly.

The job of the hands in the baseball swing is to direct the bat to the ball and transfer the power generated by the body into the ball. The goal is to keep the bat in the hitting area as long as possible with the hands flat (bottom hand palm up and top hand palm down) through the hitting area while maintaining maximum speed.

Hitting in its simplest form is seeing the ball, adjusting to the location and speed, and hitting the ball. That sounds simple but unless you have set your body in a proper position to maximize its strengths you will fail time after time.

The Batting Stance

In this section, I will discuss the ideal posture of the body that utlilizes the most energy-efficient batting stance and start-up.

Bat Selection and Grip

Bat Selection

Before engaging in battle, you must first choose the right weapon. There is no absolute formula for selecting the correct bat. However, a little common sense along with the following guidelines will ensure that you choose the best weapon for your attack on the baseball.

In determining the appropriate weight of the bat, the objective is to weigh (no pun intended) the pros and cons of bat control vs. bat weight. Don't select a bat that's too heavy and literally swings you instead of vice versa. Don't select a bat that's too light, either. In the first case, you will lose bat control. In the second instance, you will sacrifice velocity and distance (a ball hit off a Whiffle bat won't travel as far as one hit off a heavier object). Yet it is important not to sacrifice bat control for more weight.

To determine the correct length of the bat, approach home plate and take your stance. As you bend at the hips to gain balance, you should be able to extend the barrel of the bat to the outside corner of home plate. The idea here is to ensure plate coverage without crowding too close to the plate. Your size and strength also will determine the length and weight of the bat you select.

You want to make sure you can reach the outside of the plate when setting up in your stance.

Gripping the Bat

The proper grip should be one that is natural, relaxed and encourages maneuverability and fluidity. The grip shouldn't be so tight as to create muscular tension in the hands and arms. Tension tightens the body and restricts movement, the worst thing you can do for a swing. The grip should promote the maneuverability of the hands and wrist, each of which is vital to the creation of bat speed and extension of the swing. Don't squeeze the bat, simply surround the bat handle with your hands.

Grip the bat with your bottom hand first by laying the bat across the top part of the hand where the palm ends and the fingers begin. The fingers then should close around the bat naturally. Repeat the same process with the top hand and make sure that the middle knuckles on both hands are parallel to each other. This best allows the wrist joints to accelerate.

The Stance

There are three basic stances and each is designed for specific results. The best stance for you? The one that comes most naturally. Don't add unnecessary responsibilities or movements to your hitting approach simply because you want to emulate your baseball hero.

The Open Stance

This stance is most often used by the rotational (or pull hitter) for the purpose of hitting the inside pitch or to see and track the pitch more effectively. The front foot is slightly open, pointing toward the right of the pitcher, and the back toe is pointed straight toward home plate. While this stance is effective for balls thrown on the inner half of the plate, it is equally as ineffective, however, on balls thrown on the outer half of the plate because striding away from the plate causes the hips and body to fly open prematurely. Because a large majority of the pitches are thrown on the outer half of the plate, this stance is not recommended for consistent contact. However, some hitters start open to see the ball better and, as they stride, close themselves back up to being square. This style has become popular in today's game, as evidenced by the approaches of Jay Buhner of Seattle and Andres Galarraga of Atlanta.

Andres Galarraga is a prime example of the increasing popularity of the open stance.

The Closed Stance

This stance is used by players who tend to open up their hips prematurely or those who have trouble handling the pitch on the outside of the plate. This hitter starts with his front foot two to four inches closer to home plate than his back foot. The benefits of this type of stance are one-dimensional. Again, while the closed stance allows the hitter to make contact with the outside pitch more effectively, it also makes it difficult for him to hit the inside pitch because he has to swing across his body, making the rotation of the hip more difficult. The other potential problem with this stance is the hitter's vision can be impaired because he cannot see the pitch with the back eye.

This is an example of a closed stance. As you can observe, the back eye is blocked from seeing the ball.

The Square Stance

This stance is by far the most beneficial of the three. Your feet are shoulder-width apart and pointed straight toward home plate. The square stance also allows you to hit balls in all areas of the strike zone, thereby reducing a hitter's vulnerabilites. And, with this stance, the hitter can see the pitcher effectively with both eyes.

As a hitting instructor, I'm constantly trying to simplify the swing and eliminate unnecessary responsibilities in order to make learning easier for the hitter. Therefore, I recommend the square stance.

The majority of major league hitters use the square stance. Tony Gwynn provides a perfect example of the square stance.

Depth in the Batter's Box

Where should we stand in the batter's box? Usually, a pull hitter will stand deep in the box and close to the plate. This position allows him to negotiate the ball to his pull-side of the field. Yet he also simultaneously limits his offensive strategy by standing so close to the plate that he has to hit the ball too far in front of him.

The ideal, or most strategic place to stand, is deep in the box and off the plate. When your stride is completed, the front foot should land and point to the middle of home plate. With the properly balanced stance, your distance off the plate will take care of itself. The benefits of this position in the box is to cover any pitch in the strike zone. For example, if you stand too close to the plate, you will be forced to pull most pitches by casting around the ball.

A Balanced Stance

Once I asked George Brett what he thought was the most important thing about hitting that he had learned from all his years with my father. I assumed I would hear some technical explanation about the use of the hands or hips. However, George sat back and after a few moments, said simply, "Your father taught me how to swing the bat without moving my head." As simplistic as it sounds, this is the essence of hitting: To use a balanced stance and maintaining that balance throughout the swing.

Through years of research, I've found there are two elements of balance that occur in the baseball swing: One is balance in your stance before the stride occurs (static balance); the other is the remaining balance during motion (dynamic balance). Striding and swinging at a pitched baseball, starting with a good balanced stance and maintaining that same balance throughout the stride, swing and follow-through, is one of the most misunderstood and poorly taught aspects of the swing. In this section, we focus on how to successfully achieve a balanced stance with its many unique functions.

Science has provided terms to describe the dynamic functions of the body. Specifically, there are two biomechanical terms which apply to achieving balance in the baseball stance: center of gravity and athletic position. The center of gravity allows us to achieve the balance we need. But we also have to position the body's weight into an attack position. The athletic position prepares us for movement and is, therefore, critical to ensure the aggressive move toward the baseball.

Center of Gravity

If you stand up straight with your feet spread shoulder-width apart, your head centered, and you look down at the ground between your feet, you would be looking at the midpoint between your feet. This centering of your head midway between the separation of your feet ensures a balanced *center of gravity* (CG). If you take the same position and draw an imaginary line from the top of your head to your belly button, it would depict your center of gravity. So, a large part of being balanced is maintaining the center of gravity equidistant to the feet. A hitter needs to establish this balance to have an axis on which to rotate during the rotational part of the swing.

Center of Gravity

This is a shot of Bernie Williams to illustrate the center of gravity.

Athletic Position

With your feet shoulder-width apart and by standing straight up, you should feel your body weight evenly distributed between the feet. But you may also be back on your heels. And in athletics, you cannot move or attack as effectively with your weight on your heels. And you certainly can't hit from that position. Now, using the same stance, keep your legs straight and bend over slightly from your hips. You should feel your body weight moving off the heels and toward the middle and toward the balls of your feet. Now, slightly flex your knees. You should feel your position stabilize. Biomechanical scientists refer to this as the *athletic position*. You are now positioned to track and attack the ball.

Rafael Palmeiro demonstrates the athletic or balanced position.

This is how the athletic position should look. You should feel your body weight evenly distributed between the feet.

The Balanced Square Stance with Proper Plate Coverage

As you take your stance in the batter's box, you need to create balance as well as plate coverage. You can achieve both by following this simple two-step move.

1. Go to the back of the batter's box, spread your feet shoulder-width apart. While keeping your legs straight, bend over slightly from the hips and touch the outside corner of home plate with the tip of the bat. The top half of your body should lean slightly over your feet and you should feel your body weight over the balls of both feet.

2. Without raising your head or top half of your body, slightly flex your knees.

Congratulations, you now have achieved a balanced stance while ensuring plate coverage at the same time. This process should be repeated every time before taking a swing. And by doing so, it will become a habit. Let's review the benefits of the balanced stance accompanied with plate coverage.

The Benefits of the Balanced Stance with Plate Coverage

• It allows you to control movement and aggressively attack the ball.

• Bending at the hip puts your head in the most effective position to track the pitch with your eyes, and also minimizes head movement.

• It allows you to hit pitches in all areas of the strike zone.

• It establishes a solid foundation for other successful movements in the swing.

Bat Position

The swing is ultimately a sequence, from the stance to contact and to follow-through, with no one component being more important than the other. Once you've achieved a balanced stance, you need to position the bat properly.

Launch Position

The bat should be positioned where it has its greatest anatomical advantage. The path of the swing greatly affects the bat's velocity. Players start their bats in different positions but as their stride begins, the bat lands in the same destination point to allow it to swing from a 45-degree angle just off the back shoulder. This position, with the front arm across the chest, stretches the large muscles of the torso. And with the back elbow down and relatively close to the side, the hitter has the most efficient angle and strongest position from which to swing.

Notice how Mark McGwire's left arm comes across his chest. Close limbs facilitate rapid axis rotation. Also, notice how his back elbow is down!

The biomechanical law of angular momentum states: "Close limbs facilitate rapid axis rotation." This principle applies directly to the baseball swing and the golf swing. In fact, the golf swing is so closely similar to the baseball swing that one can rightfully argue that this law of momentum is equally applicable. Picture the golfer as he lifts his club away and prepares to swing toward the ball. Notice how the golfer's left arm comes across his chest and his body weight shifts to his back leg as he loads up and rotates towards the back side. These positions allow him to create leverage and power from which to strike the ball. Now imagine the golfer trying to swing with his arms away from his body. He would lose much of the power because the body is not supporting the swing.

Even in golf the principle of close limbs facilitating rapid axis rotation applies. Here's Hall of Famer Mike Schmidt showing how he can hit the long ball in golf as well.

Similarly, an ice skater rotates faster when his or her arms are close to the body. The launch position also is important because it positions the bat at the top of the strike zone and hitters should never swing at anything above their hands. This principle allows the hitter to always start the bat in the same direction when swinging at strikes.

As a hitting instructor, I constantly am trying to eliminate unnecessary responsibilities for the hitter while simplifying the approach. As you know, hitters start the bat in different positions, but this begs the question: Why? If there is a common launch position for all successful hitters, why do they add seemingly unnecessary movements prior to the launch position? Take Barry Bonds, for example. He's had a great deal of success despite his rather unusual starting position. Let me emphasize this: Just because it works for Barry Bonds doesn't mean it will help you.

Bonds is not alone with his unusual starting position There are other examples of successful hitters in the major leagues who also start with unorthodoxed bat positions. Remember, though, that they all arrive in the same launch position before swinging.

Barry Bonds has an unusual starting position, creating an extra step before getting into the launch position.

If a player is very successful starting off with an unusual bat position or stance, I do not recommend change as long as they get to the launch position in a timely manner. However, if the hitter is struggling to get to the launch position, I advise him to eliminate the unnecessary movement or get the move started sooner.

Potential Problems with Not Starting in the Launch Position

No doubt you've seen hitters such as Edgar Martinez, Barry Bonds and Gary Sheffield hold the bat with the barrel pointed toward the pitcher. You've also probably seen other hitters start with a bat position somewhere in between. Why is this a potential problem? Reaction time. See, there's only a fraction of time between the moment the pitcher releases the ball to when the hitter must get his bat ready in a proper position to launch the swing. Through endless hours of studying hitters on video tape, I've found that the greatest hitters of all time arrive in the same position to launch the swing. So if the latter is true, why create any unnecessary steps prior to having the bat ready in the launch position? There really isn't any reason, which is why I encourage hitters to simply start the bat in the proper launch position.

Yes, it's hard to argue with the success of Martinez, Bonds and Sheffield. They are able to start with their bat positions in an unusual place and then move the bat to the ideal launch position in time. But not everyone is blessed with these reflexes and quick reaction time. In other words, just because their unusual bat position works for them doesn't mean it will work for you. It is far more logical to have your bat position already set in the launch position rather than to invent another movement that could adversely affect your overall hitting. In fact, I would argue that when players such as Martinez, Bonds and Sheffield find themselves engaged in slumps, the No. 1 reason is that extra movement they must make to get their bats in the proper launch position. More often than not, when they are slumping, they are late getting started with their swing. And the culprit is that split second of time that they must adjust their bat to the launch position.

Rhythm, Movement and Triggering the Swing

OK, so now you are getting close to triggering the sweetest swing possible. Your stance is square with your feet shoulder-width apart, and you have guaranteed plate coverage by bending over from the hip, and touching the outside corner of the plate. You are slightly flexing your knees to provide a balanced stance, and you are placing your bat in the launch position. Your head is upright, thus in the best position for keeping both eyes focused on the pitcher's release point. And you are preparing to track the incoming pitch. Still, there's a pretty good chance you feel tight, right? Don't panic. I have a cure.

Just before the pitcher begins his wind-up, hitters begin to do things that most of us watching don't usually notice. See, ironically, even with the body seemingly at rest, it has a tendency to tighten up or stiffen. This is *tension.* Hitters, however, guard against tension with their own methods. These methods or rituals help to avoid the body tensing up. We'll call these methods or rituals a player's *rhythm.*

Rhythm

Watch professional tennis and pay attention to the player about to receive a serve, and notice how the player often sways from side to side or twirls the racquet. After returning a shot, you also will see the player moving his or her feet, readying to move quickly and instinctively to either side in preparation for the next return. This is the tennis player's pre-swing *rhythm or movements,* and that allows the body to relax and, therefore, react quicker.

If you watch a boxer you also might see him moving his feet from side to side, dancing around his opponent while preparing to launch his swing or punch. Or picture two drag-race cars waiting for the series of flashing lights to signal the start of a race. What are the two drivers doing to their engines? Revving them. They are conducting a rhythm with their right feet, waiting for that moment to launch. These are all examples of methods and rhythms that prepare oneself for that split second when it's time to react.

Now, picture yourself in the batter's box about to receive a 97-mph fastball from Randy Johnson. Time to get that foot on the pedal and start revving your hitting engine, don't you think? You may waggle the bat slowly forward and back or simply rock your hands slightly. This should relieve tension. The key is to avoid being slow and stiff. And whatever preswing rhythm or movement you choose to fight off tension is OK. Personalize it. And form a habit with it.

When I was a kid playing Little League I tried to emulate certain major league players' preswing rhythms. But truthfully, they never felt comfortable. I was too young and my body wasn't coordinated enough at that time to handle such movements. To be effective, the preswing rhythm must be a natural and comfortable move to the hitter because body types are as different as their levels of coordination and comfort.

In addition to allowing you to react quicker, preswing rhythm helps you maintain balance. As I indicated earlier, there are two types of balance that are a major influence in the swing. The balance in the stance is the one we have discussed. The other type of balance is called *dynamic balance* and it occurs in the stride and swing.

The Stride And Triggering Mechanism

The toughest aspect of the swing is keeping your head from moving too far forward when striding. Therefore, it is vital to discuss what happens to the position and movement of the head as the stride occurs. Your head controls where your body weight is distributed. When you stride before swinging, which is the essence of hitting, you must possess excellent balance to be able to maintain the head position equidistant between the feet throughout that stride. This is the art of dynamic balance.

45° Angle

Left Arm Across Chest

Back Elbow Down

Dynamic Balance
(Head-equidistant)

Alex Rodriguez has completed his stride. Notice his center of gravity is stationary and midway between his feet. And notice on the diagram his bat angle (45 degrees) as well as his left arm coming across his chest with his back elbow close to his side.

Because the head moves forward when you stride, you must subconsciously attempt to pull it toward your back leg. This successfully prohibits the head from traveling too far forward. In this next section I will discuss the different methods hitters utilize to maintain the head and weight toward the back side. Again, you may notice a difference in style from hitter to hitter. But the end result is the same.

The Three Types of Movements Back: Pre-Set, 50-50 and Leg Kick

The Pre-Set Method

Beside adversely affecting your pivot point for proper hip rotation, moving the head too far forward in the stride restricts the vision and tracking of the incoming pitch. The length of your stride also determines how much your head drops or moves forward. This is why you see some hitters, including George Brett, Edgar Martinez, Tim Raines, Larry Walker, Robin Ventura and Mo Vaughn pre-set their weight toward the back leg.

George Brett

Larry Walker

Robin Ventura

All three of these hitters start with their weight back. All three have remarkably similar swings and have enjoyed splendid careers.

The aforementioned players choose this particular style of starting with their weight on the back leg before striding to avoid too much movement. Simply start the position by leaning your body weight toward your back leg. This is highly recommended for younger players just getting started all the way to players in college.

The 50-50 Method

For comfort reasons, other players choose a different way of staying back. They start with the head centered between the feet prior to beginning the stride. They slightly shift their weight toward the back side as the stride foot goes forward. Fred McGriff, Cecil Fielder, and Frank Thomas are all examples of players who choose to keep their weight back in this fashion. The reasoning behind this move is to counteract the forward movement of the stride with simultaneous movement backward of the upper body (hands, head, etc.).

Alex Rodriguez

Manny Ramirez

Bobby Bonilla

Another method that helps keep your weight back is the leg raise. Here you see Alex Rodriguez, Manny Ramirez and Bobby Bonilla demonstrating various degrees of the leg raise.

The Leg Raise Method

The last style for keeping your weight back involves the high leg raise or inward knee pinch. These methods cock the hips and force the weight toward the back side. Try it yourself. Get into your balanced stance and lift your front stride knee up and hold it. Where is your weight? Where is your head? Back and back. Now, try the inward pinch. Same stance but instead of raising the knee, turn and pinch the inside of your knee slightly toward your back leg and hold it. You should have the same feeling of your weight being back. Players using this method are Juan Gonzalez, Manny Ramirez and Alex Rodriguez.

I feel this particular move is the most difficult of the three because the leg is raised so high that it doesn't always get down in time to start the approach of the actual swing. And the actual timing of the stride foot touching down is of great importance to the success of the swing.

The most important concept to remember is that these three styles are different ways of staying back. But the results are the same. Again, being comfortable when performing these swing enhancers is all that matters. Choose whatever style suits you.

The Trigger And Stride Length

With your balanced stance and your feet shoulder-width apart, you are ready to begin your stride. But before the actual stride begins, some hitters have another move called a *trigger* that stretches the big-banded muscles. Think of a rubber band being pulled and stretched back. It is this elastic-snapping motion that provides the greatest degree of velocity. We can apply this principle to hitting a baseball as well. Earlier we discussed how hitters have different starting approaches, but all arrive at the same position to swing from. And now we will discuss another example of an additional preswing tool a hitter uses to begin his stride and attack the baseball.

Hitting purists have believed there is only one trigger that occurs in the most powerful baseball swings and that it happens prior to the time the ball is released from the pitcher's hand. This trigger takes place in the hands and arms as they move back while the stride foot moves forward. Regardless of where the hitter starts his bat in the launch position, all hitters arrive at this trigger position to create bat velocity. For example, some hitters start their swing by dropping or hitching their hands down toward their waist. Then they bring their hands back up as they begin to trigger their swing. (This is not recommended for most players.) If the hitter does start near, or in, the launch position just as the ball is about to leave the pitcher's hand, the hitter moves his hands back slightly past his rear shoulder and the lead arm presses across the chest. This stretches the big-banded muscles, like a rubber band, creating anatomical leverage as the stride foot moves forward. It's important to realize that the shoulders should remain relatively square to home plate during this trigger. You should also realize that this move happens simultaneously with the stride. Caution against cocking the hands so far back that the bat is in a wrapped position with the barrel pointed toward the pitcher, or too far away from the launch position.

Earlier in the section I mentioned that the common belief has been that only one trigger in the baseball swing existed. We just thoroughly discussed the most widely recognized one – the trigger of the hands and arms. However, after thorough study of today's best hitters by using slow-motion video, I have discovered a second hidden trigger that enhances the swing that nobody has ever mentioned. And the majority of the new generation of sluggers possess this second trigger.

Here's Juan Gonzalez' unique two-trigger system. During the first trigger, his hands and arms go back slightly. During the second trigger, his front knee turns in and his back forces the hips to cock. The weight is on the back side.

The Second Trigger

As we discussed in the previous section, the first trigger is the cocking action with the hands and arms going back slightly while initiating movement and stretching the big-banded muscles as the stride foot simultaneously goes forward. The other trigger moves I detected are in the lower half of the body – in the different ways hitters use to pick up their stride leg. This causes the hips to slightly trigger back before exploding with rotation squarely through the hitting area. I propose there are actually two triggers in the swing; one that occurs in the upper body, and a second in the lower half of the body before the actual stride foot goes forward. For example, take a look at Detroit Tigers slugger, Juan Gonzalez.

Other second-trigger hitters include: Manny Ramirez, Edgar Martinez, George Brett, Frank Thomas, Raphael Palmeiro and Sammy Sosa.

These moves are the natural ways these players tap into the power of their individual bodies. I don't feel you can teach these types of moves to younger players in Little League because these are extremely difficult moves that only the most highly coordinated and developed baseball sluggers can perform on a consistent basis.

The Stride: Its Length and Execution

The width of the hitter's feet in the set-up and the length of the stride taken has been another oft-debated subject in baseball circles for years. As we discussed earlier, starting with your feet shoulder-width apart in the stance applies to all body types. Your stride should be proportionately the same, too. In other words, if you are short, your stride should be shorter than that of a taller person because of your body type. And as you will come to understand, your starting position greatly influences your ending position.

The length of the stride is going to greatly affect what the body is capable of accomplishing. As we study in the next chapter, once the stride has been completed, the hips have to slightly shift to the front heel to establish a pivot point for the most effective hip rotation. The length and time consumed in this process affects the hitter's timing and what he is capable of kinetically acheiving with his body.

During the 1950s and through the late 1960s hitters generally had narrow stances and short strides which made their hips and shoulders rotate at the same time. The shoulder rotation pulled the hands away from the hitting zone and limited the hitter to pulling the ball while also making it impossible to cover the outside part of the plate. Remember that approximatley 80 percent of pitches are thrown on the outside of the plate these days, so you can imagine the disadvantage this poses for a hitter.

To be truly effective at covering the whole strike zone, you must have separate rotations of the hips and shoulders. To best accomplish this you should start with your feet shoulder-width apart and take a shoulder-width-and-a-half stride. This distance facilitates the slight shift of the hip over the front heel, establishing the best pivot point for the hip to start its rotation. It also encourages the hands, not the shoulders, to advance toward the ball. Now I would like to discuss the pros and cons of short vs. long strides. If you are a little confused right now, don't worry. The next chapter clarifies how the hands work with the body in a step-by-step fashion.

The Long stride

As the stride foot's distance increases so does the movement of the head. This has a twofold effect. The first occurs when the head moves too far forward, resulting in a *lunge*. A lunge occurs when the head continues moving past the equidistant point of the feet, causing the upper body to move too far forward and thereby blocking the hip's rotation. As we discussed earlier, *dynamic balance* involves keeping the head equidistant between the feet when striding. The second effect occurs when the head drops down, impeding the tracking of the incoming pitch.

The Wide Stance

Another debate I've often heard concerns a stance with a wide base – your feet much wider apart than shoulder width. This stance poses a potential problem. While it prevents the head from dropping, it creates a longer distance for the hip to accomplish its proper shift to the front heel for successful rotation. This type of stance is often used as a quick fix for certain types of slumps, but we will get into that when we discuss trouble-shooting.

In terms of the wide stance, no one's gets much wider than Jeff Bagwell's. Although he's had success using it, I wouldn't recommend it to anyone else.

The Purpose of Striding

The stride forces the body and the swing to start in the correct direction. The step toward the pitcher stretches the muscles between the lower and upper body – this is called eccentric muscle action. The stretch is necessary to develop maximum power and velocity. I've often described it this way: The stride sets up a place for the body to rotate and swing. So, we always stride before swinging, never striding and swinging at the same time because we need the stride foot and heel to completely land flat on the ground before the hip can shift and begin its rotation toward the baseball. One of the interesting discoveries I've made regarding the stride is that some coaches still believe and erroneously teach players that you can keep your weight back by landing on the ball of your front foot when you stride. As I studied this concept more with kinetics in mind, I turned to another sport to evaluate this information. Go back to our golf-swing example. Picture the golfer rotating his hips and torso back, and then before he moves forward to hit the golf ball, notice his front foot. His heel is always down before he can rotate his hips properly. Try it for yourself.

Now, since you must establish the same pivot point for your hips in the baseball swing, it's only logical that you also land with the front foot and heel touching down.

Striding with the Front Toe Closed

Another important aspect of the stride is the direction of the stride and the position of the front toe when it lands. The goal of the hitter is to stay in the hitting area as long as possible while rotating and attacking the baseball, and striding with the front toe closed gives the hitter the best opportunity of doing so.

This young student keeps the front toe closed while attacking the baseball.

Once the stride foot is planted, the subsequent sequence of attacking the ball may cause the front toe to open a little, or even turn over because of the force being applied. This illustrates the need for a closed stride. Without it, the front toe winds up opening more toward the pitcher and the body's hips will fly open prematurely.

I remember, when I was growing up, lots of coaches and players thought you could stride in the direction of the pitch. So, if the pitch was inside you could stride slightly open to enhance the clearing of the hips. Or, if the pitch was outside, you could stride toward the plate as long as you didn't open up too soon. After viewing slow-motion video and with the understanding of how fast the baseball is actually traveling, it became clear to me that striding toward the pitch was poor advice. The reason? You stride before the ball is released, and therefore there is no way one can think that fast or have the time to stride where the ball is being pitched.

Important Tips To Remember

When it comes to comfort in the length of the stride, your body type is going to dictate the length of your stride. To review some important points about the stride and its distance, here are a few rules for you to remember as we finish chapter 3.

- Always start your feet shoulder-width apart and get into a habit of trying not to stride more than 1 and 1/2 shoulder-width apart to keep your dynamic balance and allow for the hip to easily establish a pivot point for rotation.

- Make sure you stride first and swing second.

- Stride straight toward the pitcher.

Chapter 4:

The Swing is the Thing: From Launch To Follow-Through

You've probably heard a million times that if you want to hit with power you need to put your hips into the swing. That is partially true, but the hands and hips must work in unison if you want to hit with power. Even the best hip rotation without proper use of the hands won't lead to success. We will discuss the relationship between the hips and the hands in launching the swing in two parts. In the first part, I will describe how the body functions when performing these particular acts of the swing. In the second part, I will describe what the hitter experiences as he executes this process.

Let's pick up where we left off from the previous chapter. Once your stride has been completed with your front foot landing flat and closed, your bat should be resting in the launch position. You should be in a balanced position with the top half of your body slightly bent over. Your legs should remain slightly flexed with your head upright and centered between your feet. You should be set to track the incoming pitch.

Here's Jim Thome completing his stride. Notice his bat in the launch position and his head centered between his feet.

At this point, you have three goals: first, taking the shortest and most direct path to the ball; second, creating as much bat velocity as possible; third, covering the entire strike zone. Your hands should be positioned above the strike zone and close to your body with your bat at a 45-degree angle. Your head should be stabilized, preparing to be an axis for rotation. Your front hip should begin to rotate, causing the back hip to also start simultaneous rotation. Your hands should now begin to pull the knob of you bat directly to the incoming pitch as the barrel of the bat stays above your hands. Although your hips start the swing, your hands should be close enough behind that you actually feel your hips and hands working in unison. While pulling the knob of your bat to the ball, you should feel as though you're switching momentum from your back foot into your front leg. The key here, remember, is to not let your head move forward.

Direct Path to the Ball

Where the knob of the bat goes, the barrel quickly follows. By pulling the knob of the bat to the ball, you are taking the shortest and most direct route, which, of course, is a straight line. You also should keep the barrel of the bat close to the trail shoulder, ready to accelerate into the incoming pitch. This is what is meant by staying inside the ball with the hand before releasing the barrel. So as the hips start to rotate in the baseball swing, the hands are pulling the knob of the bat to (or staying inside) the pitched ball. As you are rotating your hips and pulling the knob to the ball, your back heel should stay down. The heel should begin to rise as the front hip clears. The back toe should begin to pivot or turn, thus allowing the back hip the freedom to fully rotate. It is important that the back heel never reverse itself during the process, a no-no some coaches refer to as "squishing the bug." Reversing the heel is counter-productive, because it moves your body weight away from the approaching ball and forces the bat and back shoulder away from the contact area. Also, since you are starting the swing slightly above the strike zone, pull the knob forward and down to hit a strike.

This is how I teach my students. Notice him pulling the knob of the bat to the ball.

Notice how Ken Griffey Jr. and Frank Thomas pull the knob of the bat to the ball as they rotate off the back side. Also take note: They are not "squishing the bug" as most coaches teach.

Two Types of Long Swings

Logic dictates that if the knob goes up, the barrel of the bat immediately drops. This lengthens the swing and also makes the weight of the bat more difficult to manage, thus slowing down the swing. It also makes it impossible to take a level swing. This type of swing greatly decreases the opportunity for consistent contact. Many hitting coaches refer to this as a loopy or long swing.

What happens if you take the knob of the bat up? Look at how the back shoulder and the barrel of the bat drops.

The other type of long swing occurs when the bat is cast away from the body and the barrel of the bat loops around the ball before contact. There are two causes. The first is the wrapping of the bathead around the ball before the swing. This bat position makes it impossible to pull the knob, because the shoulders must overcompensate in order to get the bat back in front of the body. The second is when the top hand dominates the swing, which also causes the bat head to loop around the ball prior to contact.

Here's a perfect example of Paul O'Neil hitting with flat hands. Notice his top hand is underneath the bat. And again, he's not squishing the bug.

Backspin or Topspin?

When striking the baseball, it's important for your hands to stay flat and extend through the ball. This action creates backspin on the ball, which permits the ball to carry further. The most common flaw in most swings is when hitters roll their wrists over prematurely. This action creates topspin and subsequently causes the ball to accelerate toward the ground, much like a sinker ball darts downward for a pitcher.

Wrist joints are hinge joints and their purpose during a batting swing is to flex and extend, not roll over. When you roll over the wrists, the barrel of the bat automatically is jerked back toward your body, decreasing your extension and limiting your power.

Here's a younger player demonstrating the same technique used by O'Neil: The top hand is underneath the bat.

One of the most important elements to successful hitting deals with what the top hand does when creating bat velocity. The mistake numerous coaches have made throughout the years when describing the function of the top hand is to use the word "push." Even today, some coaches teach that the back arm and top hand should provide a powerful push forward into full extension, and then the wrists should roll over as both hands remain on the bat through the majority of the stroke.

Nothing illustrates what rolling the wrists over looks like better than this finish by Paul Molitor. Yes, Molitor had a great career. But he could have driven the ball with more backspin if he had had flatter hands.

This teaching of the "push" and "rollover" techniques makes my skin crawl for one simple reason. It doesn't work for the majority of people, and it doesn't make sense. To be fair, that technique is finally being exposed for the most part. Anyone who has bothered to study the simple laws of motion understands the technique's limitations. Think of it this way: What's usually easier in moving any item, pushing or pulling?

Like Molitor, Cal Ripken Jr. rolls his wrists over. At least with Ripken, he doesn't roll the wrists over as quickly as he used to and, therefore, he has gotten better extension in recent years.

By now you should understand that both hands should pull the knob of the bat forward and down to the ball as it is heading toward the strike zone. And don't think you can push with the top hand and pull with the bottom hand. Instead, let the bottom hand do the work, or the pulling. With the bottom hand pulling, your bat will accelerate through the zone in the quickest fashion. The top hand merely supports the pulling action, and should not inhibit velocity. The law of kinetic energy also apply to the baseball swing. The law of kinetic energy simply state that the more bat velocity you create, the more power you will achieve. And in baseball terms, that power translates into distance.

Here's an example of the pulling vs. pushing argument. Picture yourself with a wet towel in your hand about to attempt the oldest locker room prank known to man. You want to playfully whip your friend as he passes. Your bottom hand pulls the close end of the towel forward and then snaps or releases the other end, creating a bullwhip motion (velocity). If you've ever been the victim of a wet towel snap, you know how it can sting. Now try the same prank by simply trying to push the towel at your friend as if you were throwing a baseball. No whip and no velocity. And no stinging feeling for the victim.

Where to Hit the Baseball

During the swing, the objective is to aim for the inside top half of the baseball. Underline this right now. Why the inside top half? The top half should be your target because of the bat's gravity. As level as you feel you can swing the bat, gravity still will force your barrel to drop slightly before it reaches the ball. Thus, by aiming for the top half, you will improve your odds at hitting the center of the ball. It is imperative that the barrel of the bat remains above your hands in its route to the baseball.

You aim for the inside of the baseball to achieve the best swing efficiency. As we have already discussed, you want to keep your hands close to your body as you pull the knob to the ball. By aiming for the inside of the ball, the power you generate is released out and away from your body.

The first thing I do with a new student is determine how much backspin he gets when hitting the ball. I put the student in the batting cage, one that is at least 90 feet long and has enough width that I can distinguish where his hits are going.

This exercise reveals the angle of the hitter's swing and therefore how much instruction the person needs. Where the ball travels – whether he's hitting the top of the screen, one of the sides, or is bouncing groundballs – reveals something about his swing. I find this procedure the most reliable diagnostic tool anybody can have.

As a hitting instructor, I'm interested in how often the student can hit the ball in the air to the screen behind the pitcher's mound in 20 swings. Why that screen? Because a hitter has to hit the ball with the desired backspin in order to be consistent in reaching that screen.

This exercise will show me how much bat extension the hitter is getting. Is his top hand cutting off the swing prematurely? Many hitters who swing with a dominant top hand hit the back screen just four or five times in those 20 tries. Four or five times isn't acceptable. Even nine or 10 isn't good enough. With a proper swing, you should be able to hit the back screen at least 15 times. If the left part of the screen is hit or ground balls are common, the diagnosis is that the top hand is rolling over.

Pull the Knob with the Hands, Not the Shoulders

So far, we have talked of the hips and hands and their relationship to starting the swing, but there is one other rotation that occurs in the baseball swing. The shoulders also turn. Hitting coaches often instruct to keep the front shoulder "in" to prevent the shoulders from turning too soon. If you turn the front shoulder too soon, you will pull away from the ball prematurely, thus reducing your plate coverage and power.

I teach my students to focus on moving the swing by pulling the knob of the bat with the hands, not by jerking the shoulders, because the shoulders have a strong tendency to rotate too soon. Any premature rotation or turning of the shoulders intrudes on the hands pulling the knob to the ball.

Try it for yourself, but be careful when doing this. Have your friend or coach stand behind you as you take your stance, take a stride with your bat in the launch position, pause, then have your coach or friend grab the barrel of your bat with both hands firmly. Now, try to swing. If you can pull the barrel out of his hands with relative ease, your shoulders aren't pulling the bat. If you can't pull the barrel out freely, your shoulders are doing too much work and your hands aren't pulling the knob. Now switch positions with your partner, so you can feel the difference between using your hands to pull the knob of the bat and having your shoulders do the work. In chapter six I will show you specific drills to prevent your shoulders from carrying the load.

If the hitter can't pull the barrel of the bat out of my hand, he's relying too much on his shoulders to perform the swing.

Timing

The other interesting part of creating bat speed is timing. The hands should be pulling the knob of the bat before the ball gets into the strike zone or you will fail. If you don't have the knob going to the ball before is gets in the strike zone, you have no chance of producing enough bat speed to deliver a powerful blow. The next time you watch a major league game on television, pay close attention to when the hitter checks his swing. When the replay is shown to give the viewer a better look at whether the hitter has swung too far or checked his swing in time, you can also determine something else: You should see the hitter rotating and pulling the knob of the bat to the ball, then at the last moment deciding not to release the barrel of the bat. This is the best example of actually witnessing a hitter pulling the knob of the bat to the ball before the ball gets to the hitting zone.

Making Hard Contact

Now that we've established that you need to attack a baseball by rotating and pulling the knob to the ball, we need to turn our attention toward what will support this physical action. The answer? The front leg. The front leg will support you as you drive your momentum into it. While you decide where to make contact based on the pitch location, your front leg should firm up and become as stiff as possible. The front leg is just like the brakes on a bus – it initiates and absorbs the transfer of energy, throwing you forward and excelling the bat through the ball. When the front leg firms up, it virtually steers the bat head aggressively to the ball.

Alex Rodriguez checks his swing, which he could do because he had the knob of the bat going to the ball on time and was able to decide not to swing at this particular pitch.

This brings us back to a common term for hitting coaches, "squishing the bug," or keeping your weight on your back leg and rotating the back toe. While hitting coaches who preach this method may have good intentions, they don't realize that this method will keep the hitter on his back foot and thus prevent full hip rotation. To compensate, the hitter usually will try to rotate on both his hips at the same time, an impossible task. This causes the hitter to consistently force the bat around the ball prematurely, creating a long swing. The bat will get around the ball and force the hitter to pull everything, as we have indicated before. Lunging is also a danger. Lunging keeps the hips from performing their proper rotation.

Jose Cruz Jr. shows us how the front leg firms up. The front leg firms as the bat head is released into contact.

Chapter 4

Communication, Contact Area and Weight Transfer

As a coach, I believe it is imperative to have a thorough understanding of your subject in order to communicate well and get the desired results from your students.
When I see a hitter pulling the ball persistently, I know he was taught to be a back-
foot hitter. Therefore, his bat gets around the ball, making him a one-dimensional
hitter. Obviously he never was taught the importance of pulling the knob and rotating to his front side. I also can spot poor teaching methods if a hitter does not hit
with backspin.

It also is crucial to your success as a hitter to learn to hit pitches in all the areas of
the strike zone. It is important to understand where to make decisive contact for
every pitch thrown to you. It has long been taught that you should hit an inside
pitch in front of the plate, a pitch down the middle is a little further back, and an
outside pitch deeper in the back of your stance. But my research has revealed a
rather surprising discovery – that on all types of pitches you should get accustomed
to making contact a little in front of your front knee. In other words, your bat head
at the point of contact should be in fair territory, with your arms beginning to
extend (see photographs).

Understanding weight transfer – how much and on what pitches – is important in
determining how to hit pitches in all locations within the strike zone, in my opinion, this has never been discussed adequately in any hitting book. By taking the
knob to the ball regardless of where the ball is pitched, as you have learned, your
weight and energy will be directed for maximum results.

For pitches thrown on the inside part of the plate, your swing should be more rotational than on any other type of pitch. There is still full hip rotation and weight
transfer, but you should be hitting more against your front leg. You rotate to your
front leg, but it has to firm up more quickly simply because you have to release the
bat head sooner than for any other type of pitch. If you don't release the bat head
soon enough, you will be "handcuffed" or jammed, and you likely will hit the ball
on the handle, if you hit it at all. Should you release too soon, you will be making
contact already fully extended, which likely will cause you to hook or pull the ball.

The epitome of a pull hitter, Barry Bonds, pulls the ball as he becomes more rotational and hits somewhat against his front leg.

With pitches over the middle of the plate, your weight transfer is more deliberate than on an inside pitch, because you have more time to get the bat head to the ball. Ideally, your arms should be roughly three-quarters extended upon contact, allowing you to hit the ball in front of your body. Pitches in this location give you more flexibility in the direction you hit the ball. If as a right-handed hitter you get the bat head through the swing a little early, you will hit the ball to left-center field; later, and you will hit the ball to right-center field. Either way, you may well be standing on second base with a double.

Pitches thrown on the outside part of the plate give many hitters their biggest challenge. And remember, that is where many pitchers concentrate the location of their pitches. Trying to pull an outside pitch is perhaps the biggest no-no and reason for failure in hitting. Trying to pull an outside pitch, even with the best technique, often results in a weak groundball to an infielder. So for this outside location, your best chance for making consistent, hard contact is to make your most decisive weight transfer to the front leg and take the knob to where the ball is. You should still hit the outside pitch in front of the plate but with an aggressive weight transfer to the front leg you can be successful. Tony Gwynn, Wade Boggs, Manny Ramirez, Frank Thomas, Juan Gonzalez and Derek Jeter are all front-foot hitters and are all great opposite-field hitters.

Jose Cruz Jr. drives an outside pitch to the opposite field. Notice the back foot and heel almost vertical to the ground. This allows for full hip rotation and weight transfer.

Full Hip Rotation

I cannot stress enough the importance of the back foot's shoelaces ending up pointing toward the pitcher, and the heel pointed toward the sky. That is what allows the hip to fully rotate through the ball as well as what allows the hands to stay inside the pitch.

Lead-arm Extension: To Release or Not to Release

From all the research and field study I've done over the last decade, I feel I've been able to zero in on the top four all-time secrets of hitting. Drum roll please. They are:

• Taking the knob to the ball.

• Maintaining flat hands through the hitting area.

• Getting the lead arm extended through the hitting area.

• Swinging the bat through to a high finish.

These, my friends, are your stairs to baseball heaven. These are my secrets of the swing.

My father's trademark, what became known as the Lau trademark, has been to teach hitters to let go of the top hand after impact. In reality, though, I do not teach my students to let go after impact with the top hand. What I do teach is for my students to take the knob of the bat to the ball, have flat hands through the hitting area, maintain extension and wind up with a high finish. If you obey these four Lau Laws you will become a great hitter. And here's the kicker: If you obey these laws you cannot help but let go with the top hand after impact. That's right. Letting go of the top hand is not a goal, it is a verification of a correct swing.

When Mark McGwire shattered Roger Maris' single-season, home run record, *The Sporting News* magazine ran a story examining some changes McGwire had made to his swing. What the story pointed out was that the turning point in McGwire's rise from inconsistent slugger to home run legend occurred when he adopted my father's one-hand extension principle. Some baseball people claim McGwire became a great power hitter when he began to release his top hand after contact. But truthfully, he became a great hitter when he adopted the four above secrets to the swing.

A top-hand release is the result of maximum lead-arm extension and a high finish. Amazingly, the knock on the method of releasing the top hand that my father was the first to suggest more than two decades ago, used to be that it took away power. Tony LaRussa, McGwire's manager with the St. Louis Cardinals, defended my father's teaching methods for years. He disputed the notions of those old school hitting coaches who thought that my father's methods did nothing but promote soft singles to the opposite field. The truth, LaRussa argued, was that my father, who worked for LaRussa, taught line-drive hitters to use the whole park, thus making them more productive. When my father instructed a true home run hitter, like a Greg Luzinski or a Carlton Fisk or a Harold Baines, he taught them to use a slight uppercut with full extension. LaRussa, noting the distinguished home run success of McGwire, Sammy Sosa and Ken Griffey Jr. the past few years, recently said, "A lot of us who are tremendous fans of Charley Lau know now that he's up there smiling because there's a certain amount of vindication for that style of hitting he taught."

You have only to look around the major leagues to see that a top hand release is a great benefit, not a deterrent, in a player's power production. The list of top-hand devotees is impressive and long. Besides the aforementioned three, you can add to the list of sluggers such players as Juan Gonzalez, Tino Martinez, Fred McGriff, Manny Ramirez, Dante Bichette, Tony Clark, Andres Galarraga, Frank Thomas, Jim Edmonds, David Justice, Shawn Green and Todd Walker. And that's just a small sampling. What these players have in common is that they all have or can hit more than 30 home runs in a season.

One guy in my opinion who could easily join that list because of his great natural hitting skills is Tony Gwynn, arguably the best hitter for batting average since George Brett. Gwynn routinely has won batting titles. I have a great respect for his ability to put the bat on the baseball. However, Gwynn, while weighing in at 230 pounds, has yet to hit for much power. From what I have seen, he has excellent fundamentals except for his tendency to roll over his top hand prematurely. That doesn't permit him to get through the ball with flat hands and causes him to lose extension. That has limited his power. Gwynn and I have discussed this subject at length and he readily agrees he should have more power for a guy his size. And for a while after we talked, particularly in 1997, it seemed as if he was addressing that aspect of his hitting. His power production went up 17 home runs. Gwynn once appeared at a South Florida baseball camp I coordinated and told the kids that my father's teaching philosophy had been instrumental in his advance as a hitter. But later in a television interview, when asked if he practiced my father's Absolutes of

Hitting, he replied, "I use most of them, but not all of them." That statement bothered me. So in the car on the way back to his hotel, I asked him just which of the 10 Absolutes he disagreed with. After a long silence, he confessed, "You got me Charley. I'm sorry."

The point here is certainly not to knock Gwynn for his lack of public acknowledgment of all of my father's Absolutes of Hitting. Nor am I criticizing him or his lack of power. The point is that even a great hitter like Tony Gwynn can have an aspect of his swing that could use improvement.

How Do I Get Lead-Arm Extension?

Keeping the bat as flat as you can for as long as you can has two effects. It allows you to expose the sweet spot of the bat in and through the hitting area longer and adds about 15 to 20 mph to your bat velocity. The other obvious challenge in hitting a baseball is that you are trying to hit a round object with a round bat, and do it squarely.

Through countless hours of working with swings of all types, my biggest breakthroughs have come when teaching my students the value of getting lead-arm extension in the swing. What gets the message through ultimately is the evidence: How much further the ball carries when lead-arm extension is performed properly.

The scientific reasoning behind using lead-arm extension is that the length of a lever determines the amount of leverage you can achieve. In the baseball swing, your front arm is the longer lever, and therefore it will provide more leverage and power. And this is why I preach that you shouldn't roll your wrists over prematurely because it keeps you from a flat swing that allows for extension.

Try this experiment: Extend both hands to the direction of where you would hit the ball. Which arm appears longer? And that brings us to another question: What is the function of the top hand after contact? We know that it has a tendency to roll over, rather than extend. Does it push? What if you let it go and let it slide off after contact? You will notice that your lead arm continues through the swing with much greater extension. I frequently call this a one-piece swing. If you roll over your top hand before the lead arm gets extended, it would be a two-piece swing.

Notice how the lead arm is longer and can extend further or stay flat longer than the top hand.

Finishing High

As you begin to experiment with lead-arm extension, look for your lead arm to fully extend and finish at or above the front shoulder. As you start to perfect full extension of your lead arm, you will consistently finish high, and you will begin to release your top hand naturally. By practicing off the batting tee, you will become more comfortable with the release. Once you get into a game, the release will come naturally. And even if you decide to keep two hands on the bat or if your top hand doesn't always come off, at least through a high finish you will get much better extension than you ever would without this technique. A good example is Reggie Jackson, one of the game's better power hitters of all time. My dad worked very hard with Reggie during the 1980 season, constantly reminding him to take his top hand off the bat in batting practice. Reggie didn't feel comfortable doing that in a game for some reason. However, by practicing bat extension and taking the top hand off in batting practice, he kept his top hand from being too dominant when he kept two hands on the bat during games.

That year Reggie had 41 home runs and hit .300 for the first and only time in his career. Previously a predominant pull hitter, he stroked 20 of his home runs to the opposite field. Reggie finished second that year in the Most Valuable Player voting. He was beaten out by Kansas City's George Brett, another one of my father's pupils who hit .390 that season. Therefore, if you happen to be a two-handed, follow-through hitter who can't seem to change, at least you should practice releasing that top hand when hitting off the batting tee. Once you understand the dynamics of it, perhaps, as was the case with Reggie, you will prevent your top hand from being so dominant.

Dry Swing

The best way to get the feel of lead-arm extension is through a drill I developed called the *dry swing.* If you are a right-handed hitter, place the palm of your right hand on the inside of your left wrist loosely. In this position, do a practice swing, releasing the right hand when you swing through the contact area. This should assure your bottom hand maximum extension and follow-through. Left-handed hitters do the opposite – put your left hand on your right wrist. You should start to feel increased bat velocity. In fact, you may even hear the bat whistle through the zone as you swing. This drill is instrumental in developing a one-piece swing.

To start the dry-swing drill, place your top hand on the inside of your left wrist.

As you start the swing, the top hand stays on the inside part of the left wrist.

Let the top hand slide off the left wrist.

Nearing the finish, you extend that lead arm.

At the finish, you should have excellent lead-arm extension.

Open Top Hand

Here's another drill for the top hand that will help allow for maximum lead-arm extension. Grip the bat normally with the bottom hand and leave the top hand open, positioning the bat in the middle of the palm. Now take your normal swing. You should get a feel for the increased bat velocity now that the top hand doesn't dominate your swing. This is a breakthrough drill, I believe, and one you should use during the rest of your career. It provided the impetus for Alex Rodriguez to launch not only a major league career, but to win a batting title.

Start out using this drill in a batting cage with a tee. Eventually you should use it during soft-toss drills (pepper drills) and, ultimately, in live batting practice. To help prevent top-hand dominance, think about reaching out with your top hand for a paycheck every time you swing the bat, just as you are about to hit the ball.

I've witnessed students take as few as five or six swings before noticing amazing results, such as the batted ball zipping through to the back of the cage with back-spin. It's a moment of significant awakening. You won't think you've cured cancer, but I guarantee it will be a special discovery in your baseball career.

The dry swing drill simply allows you to feel the added speed in your swing. Remember: Until you get the same kind of velocity on your swing in the batting cage as you get with the dry swing, you won't hit the back of the cage with backspin with much consistency.

The open top-hand drill: Make sure you hold the bat with the top hand open when doing this drill off the tee.

Here's how you position your top hand.

Here's a student demonstrating the open top-hand drill. Notice how he releases the top hand after contact.

The ball being hit with backspin shoots back through the middle and hits the back of the screen. The flight of the ball never lies.

A student finishes his swing with excellent lead-arm extension.

I remember recently working with one hitter – John Finn, a second baseman moving up in the Chicago White Sox organization – who had the typical two-piece swing. He kept two hands on the bat, yet could stay inside the ball and be fairly consistent in hitting the back screen. His problem? The ball wasn't being hit with much authority. No rocket shots. No sizzle.

Once I showed him how to get bat extension through the release of the top hand after contact, he began punishing the ball. I remember his minor league teammates watching and simply gawking in amazement. One of them said while shaking his head, "He looks like a new man."

That's the way it happens by taming the top hand's dominant tendencies. Releasing the top hand opens the way for increased power and a consistency you likely have never experienced. All of that adds up to more confidence.

If you have no one to work with you in the batting cage, don't worry. While your education may be more fun with someone to watch you advance, it is not mandatory. You can self-evaluate because the flight of the ball never lies.

Remember that statement: The flight of the ball never lies. That fact allows you to grade your own work at any time. Watch what the ball is doing. For example, if you hit the ball on the ground, you've used your top hand too much and rolled over prematurely. If you're a right-handed hitter and you hit the ball to the left part of the screen, you got around the ball instead of driving through it. Now, if you're hitting the ball to the back of the screen with backspin, you are on your way to success. Another quick point: The tee drill should be a fixture in your hitting schedule, even after you think you've mastered everything there is to master in my system. There are major leaguers who hit off the tee every day before games, and even on their days off. Tony Gwynn works diligently at his fundamentals by hitting hundreds of balls off the tee every day.

Look for that true backspin to the back of the cage and understand this: the batting tee is the best hitting coach you will ever have. Don't wait until you have a problem to use it. Use it, so you won't have a problem.

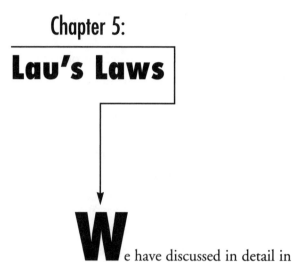

Chapter 5:
Lau's Laws

We have discussed in detail in previous pages my hitting practices. Now, let's turn those practices into law. Here are Lau's Laws on hitting, which you'll find extend beyond the Absolutes of Hitting that my father began teaching almost three decades ago.

Lau's Law No. 1:
Use a Balanced and Workable Stance.

Quite simply, to hit a baseball, you have to see it. And to see it, you must use a balanced stance that will allow you to work your hip rotation and weight transfer while also allowing your head (and eyes) to track the baseball. That's why this is Lau's Law No. 1. All the instruction and all the ability in the world won't much matter if you're employing an awkward stance that deters your head from tracking the baseball. If you can see the ball and track it, chances are you can hit it.

Lau's Law No. 1

Lau's Law No. 2:
Use a Proper Grip.

It's always been amazing to me how few instructors emphasize the grip. Yet the proper grip is critical to the swing. A bad grip can stiffen the wrists and dramatically decelerate bat speed. You must grip the bat with your finger knuckles aligned with each other on each hand. This promotes flat hands and lead-arm extension.

Lau's Law No. 2

Lau's Law No. 3:
Get Your Weight Back Before Striding.

To get your weight going forward, you must first get it back prior to striding. Think of your body as a rubber band or a sling shot. There are three ways you can accomplish this: first, you can pre-set your weight back, which I recommend because it is the easiest to accomplish; second, you can pinch your front knee toward your back knee, which is a good technique to ensure that your weight will be back; or, third, you can start at a 50-50 weight balance, and then slowly shift your weight toward your back side. But make no mistake, you must have that weight back before you start to stride.

Lau's Law No. 3

Lau's Law No. 4:
Start Your Bat in the Launch Position.

Yes, I have harped on this subject, but it's only because I believe in eliminating unnecessary steps, thus making hitting as easy and instinctive as possible. As I have conceded, some great hitters are able to start their bats in unusual positions before ultimately arriving in the launch position. But these hitters are exceptions. And they're already in the major leagues. You're not. So save yourself some aggravation and start with your bat already poised in the launch position. It saves time and energy.

Lau's Law No. 4

Lau's Law No. 5:
Stride With Your Front Toe Closed.

Keeping your front toe closed (pointed toward the plate) promotes excellent hip rotation from the back side toward a firm front side. By thinking of striding with the front toe closed, you create a more firm front side, which, in turn, makes it more conducive for your body to pull the knob of the bat toward the ball.

Lau's Law No. 5

Lau's Law No. 6:
Maintain Flat Hands Through the Swing.

By flat hands, I mean having one palm up, one palm down. The lead hand's palm should be down and the back hand's palm should be up. These are flat hands. And using flat hands through the swing and through the point of impact will create backspin on the baseball. Yes, we want backspin, because balls hit with backspin travel farther than balls hit with topspin. Ever wonder why tennis players love topspin? Because they're trying to bring the tennis ball down as quickly as possible inside the playing surface and inside the baseline. That's what topspin will do. Tennis players don't care about distance. Baseball hitters do.

Lau's Law No. 6

Lau's Law No. 7:
Keep Your Head Still and Eyes Down.

As I've mentioned before, the greatest swing in the world won't do a hitter much good if his head is moving all over the place and his eyes have darted off and are peering toward the bleachers. At the point of impact, your head must be still and your eyes must be fixed down. A "still" head allows the center of your body to act as an axis, which, in turn, creates the ideal hip rotation.

Lau's Law No. 7

Lau's Law No. 8:
Use a Fluid, Tension-free Swing.

Ever see someone really try to muscle up and power a ball? Chances are, they rarely even make contact. The reason is, tension dramatically slows down a swing in any sport — baseball, tennis, golf, you name it. The more relaxed your muscles are, the more quickly your body reacts and moves. When your body and your swing are free of tension, you increase your bat speed and velocity.

Lau's Law No. 8

Lau's Law No. 9:
You Must Have Lead-arm Extension and a Good Finish.

This is mandatory. This is what my system of hitting is all about. The lead-arm extension is vital to completing the full hip rotation. And this is what allows us to take advantage of our transfer of energy. That is why I tell my students to concentrate on a good finish. By finishing with the proper lead-arm extension, you will take advantage of every ounce of energy you have generated during the course of the swing. If you don't finish, you will cut short this transfer of energy and hinder your performance.

Lau's Law No. 9

Lau's Law No. 10:
Employ Solid Practice Habits.

Hey, not everyone was born with most major leaguers' raw ability. But even the great major leaguers practice much harder than you'd think. The more you practice, the more natural your swing will become to you. Through practice comes habit. And a great swing is a great habit to have.

Lau's Law No. 10

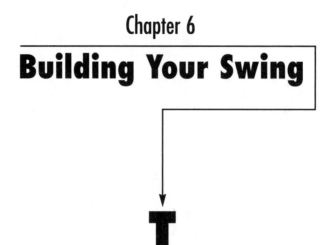

Chapter 6
Building Your Swing

This chapter is devoted entirely to building the perfect swing. We will accomplish this by describing the necessary mechanical fundamentals to build the swing, and we'll accompany the language with a series of drills designed to transform these fundamentals into habit. So where do we start in building the swing? Easy. The hands. Everything starts with the hands.

Hands-on Training

You start with the hands because the hands deliver the bat to the ball. It is through the hands and through hip rotation that you can create bat velocity. What you need to remember about the hands is this: The lead hand creates bat speed while the back hand can slow down bat speed if it begins to dominate during the swing. You need both hands to pull the knob of the bat toward the ball, which is what accelerates the pace of the bat. The reason I came up with the open top-hand drill is to ensure that the top hand doesn't dominate during this process.

Drill No. 1: Open Top Hand

In the old-school philosophy, instructors believed that the top hand should cling onto the bat like a death grip. It was believed by followers of this philosophy that it was the top hand that created power by pushing itself through the swing. So naturally, these instructors preached that you should never let the top hand off the bat. This, by physical law, forced a hitter to roll over his wrists as he pushed the bat through the hitting zone. This is a no-no.

Here's how you position your hand in the open top-hand drill.

Next, take a swing in this position.

At the point of contact, your hands should look like this.

The top hand slides off
here and you finish
your swing.

By keeping your top hand on the bat through the swing and rolling over the wrists, you create all kinds of undesirable results, most noticeably topspin on the baseball. Topspin, like a topspin lob in tennis, brings the ball back to earth more quickly. But in baseball, we want distance, which is why I preach to hitters to create backspin.

To create backspin, we must "tame" the top hand. In other words, we must make sure the top hand doesn't become dominate during the swing. We must make sure the hands and wrists don't roll over during the swing. To tame the top hand, I have come up with a drill in which hitters get into their normal stance and grip the bat accordingly. But then I tell the hitter to open the top hand as he grips the bat. By opening the top hand, the hitter is forced to concentrate on pulling the knob of the bat with both hands. Because the top hand is open and not gripping the bat, it cannot dominate or push.

What does this accomplish? Without the top hand's influence, both hands allow the bat to be released with maximum velocity. This promotes the most important aspect of hitting: lead-arm extension. You will be astonished at how quickly the bat now zips through the hitting zone. This is bat acceleration, my friends. I have had students, amateurs and professionals, who are amazed at the how much acceleration their bat suddenly possesses after this simple drill.

I always start the drill off the tee and later move into soft toss. Practice this open top-hand drill repeatedly before moving onto soft toss. Eventually, progress toward live pitching, using the same open top-hand drill.

Drill No. 2: No Feet, No Shoulders

The purpose of this drill is to emphasize the importance of the hands. You do not pull the knob of the bat to the ball by using your shoulders. If you try to use your shoulders to perform this act, you most likely will flail your left shoulder out too quickly, opening it up too soon, and thus forcing the barrel of the bat to hit around or across the ball. This will result in numerous, harmless ground balls to the shortstop, if you're a right-handed hitter, or a reduction in bat velocity.

Here's the starting position for the no-feet-no-shoulders drill. Assume a post-stride position.

Keep your shoulders square as you pull the knob of the bat to the ball. And keep your feet flat on the ground.

Here is where you should release the top hand. Notice the feet flat on the ground.

Finish the swing in this manner. Notice how relatively square my shoulders are.

The no-feet-no-shoulders drill will teach you the value of keeping your front shoulder in, and the importance of letting your hands do the work. To accomplish this drill, you keep your feet in their original stance and also keep your shoulders still. Simply concentrate on using your hands and not your shoulders to pull the bat toward the ball on the tee.

In every drill we do, we do the open-hand drill. It's no different here. We don't want top-hand dominance, and we want to keep the shoulders square to the plate.

Drill No. 3: Pull the Bat Away From Me

This is a drill I use to determine if you're truly using both hands to pull the knob of the bat to the ball instead of your shoulders. What I do as an instructor is hold the barrel of the bat with my left hand and put my right hand on the top of the hitter's head as he preps to swing. Now, this can be a dangerous drill for the instructor if not performed with caution. But by holding the barrel of the bat and then telling the hitter to conduct his normal swing, I can determine if he is using both hands, and not his shoulders, to pull the bat. If he is conducting the proper swing, he should be producing enough bat speed to rip the barrel of the bat away from my hand. If he can't rip the barrel of the bat away from me, his shoulders are inhibiting the swing. This is an awakening for the hitter because he realizes how much bat velocity he loses by pulling with his shoulders as opposed to pulling with his hands.

Here is how this drill looks to determine if the hitter is pulling the knob of the bat with his hands or his shoulders.

The Other Poison: Back-foot Hitting

We have discussed in length one of the most poisonous teachings of the old school philosophers — top-hand dominance and rolling over the wrist. There is another poison associated with this outdated philosophy equally as paralyzing to the swing: back-foot hitting. Most hitting instructors have taught back-foot hitting over the years as a deterrent to lunging at the ball. The theory had been that by keeping your weight constantly on your back foot you could prevent yourself from lunging at the ball. That much is probably true. Keeping your weight on your back foot will block most attempts at lunging at the ball. But the problem is that back-foot hitting doesn't allow you physically to take the knob of the bat to the ball.

Jim Thome is most of the time a classic back-foot hitter. He's rare, though, because there are times he does come off his back side and drives the ball to left-center field.

By sitting on your back side, it is impossible to cover the entire strike zone because the front leg firms up too soon. This forces the bat away from the body and away from the ball, creating a consistently long swing. That prevents you from hitting pitches from the middle part to the outside part of the plate, which is where most pitchers like to pitch anyway. Whatever energy is stored remains stationary on the back side. Wasted. It is the transfer of energy to cover the entire strike zone as well as fully rotate the hips.

Here's how it looks when a youngster collapses his back foot.

Back-foot hitters are notorious pull hitters. And there is a simple explanation. Without the freedom of weight transfer, they loop their swing around the ball, often making contact on the ball where 12 to 3 o'clock would be on a watch dial. That's what hooks the ball and directs it to the left side (for a right-handed hitter). Ideally, you want to hit the ball squarely in the 6 to 9 o'clock range, which allows you to direct the ball to any part of the field.

Drill No. 4: The Crossover Step

So how do we discourage hitters from becoming back-foot hitters? Through a drill I call the crossover step. Start in your normal batting stance somewhat behind the front of the tee. Now, simply take your front foot and cross over your back foot. Then move your back foot back behind your front foot and become square again in a balanced hitting position. Again, make sure your top hand is open. Then reverse the process. Take your back foot and cross over your front foot. Step first, and then proceed with your swing. This should give you the momentum to rotate off your back side and perform the correct weight transfer. It's a simple step technique, sort of like learning the cha-cha.

Here's the conclusion to the crossover-step drill. I cross over with my back foot and then get back into position.

Swing with the top-hand open. This helps to encourage weight transfer and getting that weight off the back side.

What does this prove? And how does it help? It promotes the transfer of weight and energy, which is vital to my hitting system. As you transfer your weight and energy through this drill, you will immediately notice one development. You will make a positive and aggressive move back toward the baseball. This is precisely what we want to achieve.

By the transfer of weight through hip rotation and energy transfer, we are setting up a detonation, so to speak. That detonation comes at the point of impact. All that weight and energy transfer will flow into the point of impact. And once your front side and front leg stiffen, the energy will be whiplashed toward the ball at the point of impact. Again, the point of this drill is to discourage hitters from retaining all their weight and energy on their back foot at the point of impact. Keeping that energy back makes absolutely no sense. You may store it on the back side, but then release it through a transfer. This is the best drill ever designed to encourage weight transfer.

Don't Make Heads Turn

Another key element in the fluid Lau swing is keeping the head still. The head becomes a crucial portion of my teaching because it must act as the axis from which the rest of the body turns and rotates. Think of your head as the top of the point of an umbrella. From the top of your head to the point straight below it to the ground should always remain in a straight line, just as would the center stand of an umbrella. As everything else may whirl around like an umbrella twirling, the center stand remains straight. So, if you can keep your head in that alignment, you can help promote proper rotation. If you yank your head out of that alignment, the rotation will naturally go askew, just as if you had bent the umbrella's center stand. As the body moves laterally during the course of the swing, the head moves laterally in a parallel fashion.

Drill No. 5: Quieting the Head

The best drill to ensure a hitter is maintaining a still or quiet head is to assume a post-stride hitting position. Your legs are slightly flexed and your bat is in the launch position. You're going to swing from this position without striding. This should force you to use the lower half of the body and your hands without lateral movement forward of your head. That keeps it from rotating. Make the head serve as an axis. But through repetition, the hitter will gradually train himself to keep his head motionless and in a perpendicular line with the center of his body as he progresses through the swing. That line starts at the center of the head and shoots straight down through his navel and then at the center point between his feet.

Step 1 — Assume the post-stride position with your bat in the launch position and your knees slightly flexed.

Step 2 – While keeping your head still, rotate off your back side while pulling the knob to the ball.

Step 3 – Extend through the ball with flat hands as your front leg firms up.

Step 4 – Let the top hand slide off after it extends.

Step 5 – Observe the proper finish and follow-through to the swing.

Drill No. 6: Soft Toss

Another valuable technique in teaching the Lau System is through a drill known as soft toss. Basically, I stand about 30 to 35 feet from the hitter and pitch the baseball at about three-quarter speed. Because the majority of our drills have been devoted to using the tee when swinging, we now must acclimate the hitter to live pitching. Rather than expose the hitter immediately to blistering fastballs, which might overly discourage him, I prefer an intermediate step. Soft toss. This serves two purposes: It begins to condition the hitter to using his new swing against the pitched baseball, and it also helps to build confidence because the ball is moving at a more adaptable speed.

Even with soft toss, though, we still utilize many of the same drills we have just discussed. For example, the no-feet-no-shoulder drill. The hitter should be in his normal stance and as the soft toss is thrown at him, he should deliver his swing without moving his feet and without using his shoulders. This step teaches the hitter to pull the knob of the bat to the ball by predominantly using his bottom hand and lead arm. You might be wondering if the top hand has any purpose at all during the swing. It does. The top hand's primary function is to provide support for the bat through the swing, and that is an important function. You can steer a car with one hand on the wheel, but you're still better off using two for better control of the steering wheel. The top hand in a baseball swing simply provides better control of the bat. But it should never take control of the swing. If it does, bat velocity will be inhibited.

The true value of the soft toss drill is that it introduces the hitter to timing; when to start the swing, and when to start pulling the knob of the bat. In this same drill, I also will ask the hitter to employ the open top-hand drill, which provides the hitter with his first experience of true, accelerated bat speed. This is usually when you get your first smile from the student: They are often surprised at the increase in bat speed and the pace of the ball after they make contact.

The Reward and Validation

As an instructor trying to fight the old school philosophy, it can often be trying emotionally to spot rewards. But those rewards are there in my teaching. I can remember a student not long ago who, shall we say, was not exactly blessed with the greatest athletic ability. We are not talking cobra-like reflexes. It was serious work just to get this student to swing the same way two straight times. But we labored through the drills and I was impressed with his dedication to keep trying. Yet by the time he left my school on hitting, I wasn't exactly convinced he had successfully adopted many of my teachings and principles.

But one day, a few months after he had completed my school, I happened to be sitting at a Little League game when this former student of mine came up to the plate. Naturally, I perked up and watched him carefully as he entered the batter's box. Remember, this is a young boy with very marginal athletic ability who also didn't appear to be grasping the concepts of my hitting system, at least so I thought. But on the second or third pitch, he mashed a line drive in the gap and legged out a triple. He had pulled the knob of the bat through the zone with his bottom hand, exhibited beautiful lead-arm extension, and really belted one. I looked at his face as he stood resting with one foot on the third-base bag. As he met eyes with parents in the stands, his face was positively beaming. His parents smiled. I couldn't help but smile myself.

Yes, there are rewards like this that keep instructors going. But for me, who is fighting to tear down the old-school philosophy, this was more than a reward. This was a validation. Nothing can top that.

Chapter 7

The Five Most Common Flaws in the Swing

This one's for you, coach. It's one thing to teach a system such as mine; it's another to fine-tune it when problems occur. Consider this chapter your guide to trouble-shooting. I've identified the five most common flaws in the swing that should help you to more easily identify a problem and then quickly seek the proper solution. And remember, overcoaching can seriously retard a hitter's growth.

You Can't Fix Everything

When hitters enter slumps, which all hitters eventually do, the reason is not always mechanical. Sometimes it's as simple as hitters not swinging at good pitches. Learn the strike zone. Swing at strikes. If the hitter doesn't swing at strikes, no swing will be effective. Remember, you can't put a good swing on a bad pitch.

That's why I'd like to pass on a few words of advice for all coaches and hitting instructors: Look for simple solutions first because too much analysis creates paralysis. Sometimes hitters get caught in slumps simply because their mental approach is off. That's a topic we'll get into in a later chapter on strategy and situational hitting. But for now, just remember to look for mechanical flaws, yet don't obsess with them. If there is an obvious mechanical flaw that needs to be addressed, get to it. And that's why I've come up with the five most recognizable flaws to spot.

Flaw No. 1: Bad Stance, Unorthodox Launch Position

One of the most common flaws to look for is right at the start: The hitter may no longer be ready in a balanced, workable stance, or he may be using an unorthodox launch position. In most cases, this prevents the hitter from starting on time. And if the hitter is late with the swing (pulling the knob of the bat to the ball), he will have to compensate in some other fashion that disrupts the fluid motion of the swing. He compensates just to catch up to the ball, and most likely he will violently yank his shoulders in an attempt to get the bat through the zone quicker. And as the shoulders fly open too soon, he's likely to pull his head further away from his hands and the hitting zone. It's hard to hit what you can't see.

Here's a little leaguer starting with his hands too high and a little too far away from his body. As he strides, he will be forced to drop his hands and his bat, and his left arm will drop across his chest before he can swing. Also, because his stance is upright, his head will drop and move forward, affecting his vision when tracking the incoming pitch.

Here's Edgar Martinez in the same position as the little leaguer. When Martinez struggles, it's usually because he can't get back to the launch position in time.

As you know, timing is the most important element in hitting a baseball. It is the pitcher's mission to mess with your timing, and he will do so by changing speeds or changing the pace of his delivery motion. And there are many things a hitter can do himself to mess up his own timing, most notably by using a crazy launch position.

Some people might argue that I'm infringing on a hitter's individuality when I suggest that he start in the proper launch position, rather than starting with the bat cocked in an unusual manner and *then* returning in the launch position. By teaching my students to all start in the same launch position, am I trying to create clones? Guilty as charged. But there's a sound reason for this. I'm simply trying to eliminate unnecessary steps. This one unnecessary step — starting in an unorthodox bat position and then returning to the proper launch position — does more to mess up a hitter's timing than any other flaw I've known.

The problem with many students is that they want to emulate their heroes. They see Edgar Martinez and Barry Bonds and they want to hit like them. So they start by trying to look like them. But these players are blessed with tremendous athletic and reflex ability. You might not be. Some of these hitters get away with starting in a crazy launch position because their reaction time is sufficient enough to get back to the proper launch position without hindering their timing. But I will argue this: When players such as Bonds enter slumps, the primary culprit is getting started too late. And more times than not, this occurs because of that extra step involved in the swing — the return to the proper launch position. Yes, Bonds is an exceptional talent and big-time major leaguer. But how much better would he be if he eliminated that extra step? Would he perhaps avoid some slumps? I believe the answer is yes.

Look at it this way: There are enough obstacles for a hitter to face while trying to be successful. The pitcher is doing everything possible to mess with your timing anyway, so why give him even more ammunition by messing up your own timing? Unorthodox launch positions, as cool as they might look, serve only to slow a hitter down. They also require extra energy, and that energy is simply wasted. What I'm trying to do is to make hitting as simple as possible. Hitting is tough enough. Don't add to the challenge.

Flaw No. 2: Starting Too Late

If the hitter is already starting with the bat in the launch position, but his timing is still off and he appears to be compensating to catch up to the ball, he simply isn't starting his stride soon enough. Sounds simple enough, but you'd be amazed at how many hitters or instructors don't make this connection when trying to fix a slump.

Let me give you an example. Not long ago when I was working with Alex Rodriguez of the Seattle Mariners, I went to watch him play one night at the Kingdome in Seattle. He endured a hitless night in four at-bats and the next morning we sat and watched a video of his at-bats to perhaps spot a flaw. During one at-bat, Rodriguez fouled a pitch straight back to the backstop. As we watched this, he turned to me and said, "See. I was right on that pitch. I fouled it straight back." But I rewound the tape and looked at it again and told him, "Hey, A-Rod. You want to bet your next paycheck that you actually started late on that pitch?" He was skeptical, but after we looked again, we noticed that he had started his stride late, just a fraction of a second too late. But enough to make him miss hitting the ball squarely.

That night in a game against the Royals, Rodriguez vowed to start his stride sooner. And with just that small adjustment, he socked two home runs against the Royals. No, he didn't turn over his next paycheck to me. But he did take me out to dinner that night.

The point here is that getting started in time is critical. So when should a hitter start his stride? When the pitcher's lead leg hits the ground. That's what I teach. Through the years there have been many theories on when the hitter should start. The one I remember most is the catchy phrase "When the pitcher shows his rear end, show him yours." In other words, when the pitcher turns his back side to deliver the ball, you begin your motion as well. But this is too soon and the hitter likely will become susceptible to off-speed pitches and thus began lunging at many balls. By waiting until the pitcher's lead leg hits the ground, you're gauranteed that any deceptive pitching motion is over. Once his leg hits the ground, his arm has to come forward. That's the time to get started.

Chapter 1

Flaw No. 3: Staying on the Back Side Too Long

This flaw happens to be another pet peeve of mine and it involves the teaching by many old school philosophers who insist that hitters keep their weight on their back side as they swing. The theory had been that by keeping the weight back you can prevent yourself from lunging at the ball. I'll concede this much to the theory: Yes, it will prevent you from lunging at the ball. Will it help you become a better hitter? Not a chance.

What staying on the back side or back-foot hitting does is make you a dead pull hitter. Because your front leg is constantly firming up too soon on pitches from the middle to the outside part of the plate, you can't cover the plate. Your swing becomes "long" — it drifts away from your body and winds up striking the ball on the outside. If the ball was a watch dial, you'd be striking it consistently at 2 o'clock. Naturally, hitting the ball in this position will hook the ball to the left if you're a right-handed hitter. Back-foot hitters are most susceptible to outside pitches because their hips open up prematurely and their bat head is forced away from the body. The hands don't stay in the hitting area long enough to cover outside pitches. To hit outside pitches, back-foot hitters must reach and virtually "throw" the bat just to make contact. They are thus in no position to drive the ball and the result is usually a foul ball or a weak groundout.

Notice how the back heel is not up and the shoelaces are not pointed back toward the pitcher. This is what prohibits full hip rotation.

Without the ability to cover the plate (hitting pitches in any location in the strike zone), back-foot hitters lose the potential to drive the ball to the opposite field. In the Lau system, the hitter can cover a pitch anywhere on the plate simply by making adjustments in the rotation and weight transfer, which determines when the front leg is firmed up. For an inside pitch, when you want the barrel of the bat through the zone quicker, your front leg has to firm up sooner. This is done basically by slamming on the brakes during your rotation. You pull the knob of the bat more quickly, your rotation quickens and ultimately your front leg firms up quicker. That is what I mean by slamming on the brakes. Your front leg becomes the brake pedal and it firms up, pulling the energy behind it, toward it. Now, for an outside pitch, you simply do the opposite. You start later and hit the brakes later. Back-foot hitters, on the other hand, never get proper rotation, as we have discussed before. They basically start off with the brakes already on. Try that while driving your car sometime and see how little speed you can generate. Even worse, with the front leg basically firmed up at the same time everytime, the back-foot hitter can't make any adjustments in rotation and thus is vulnerable to many pitch locations.

Notice the better action of the back heel, which now allows for better and more complete hip rotation.

And what really handicaps the back-foot hitter is the subsequent loss of power because of the lack of proper rotation and weight transfer. In the Lau system, hitters can really drive the ball because they store energy on their back side and then transfer that weight and energy during the swing. The energy is ultimately released with full hip rotation and that energy is zipped into the ball at the point of contact. But the back-foot hitter is taught to keep his weight and energy back. All that weight and energy is stored on the back side but never released. It is wasted. Back-foot hitters truly deprive themselves of driving the ball and hitting with their most power potential.

Flaw No. 4: Trying to Muscle the Ball

You've seen it a million times: A hitter trying to hit a home run by flexing his muscles and trying to knock the seams off the baseball. Nope, it doesn't work that way. In fact, the more you try to muscle up and hit a baseball, the more likely you are to miss it entirely. Muscling up or tensing up your muscles does nothing but slow down your swing and your bat speed. Bat speed is what creates velocity at the point of impact, and that velocity is what will determine the distance you hit a ball.

Muscling up to hit is probably evidenced most during slow-pitch softball games. But you can spot variations of muscling up in baseball, too. If you see someone with a two-part swing, you're witnessing a slow swing. Two-part swings are characterized by the swing breaking off into a second part once the wrists roll over, which is what most muscle hitters do. Two-part swings get no extension, by definition, because the swing is cut off as the wrists roll over — the swing rolls over at that point as well. Muscle hitters tend to have top-hand dominance, because they're trying to power the ball. And you know by now what top-hand dominance does — it forces the wrists to roll over. The point is, trying to muscle the ball creates a slow, two-part swing that has little chance of driving the ball.

What has happened in baseball today is that as more hitters become addicted to the weight room and beef up their upper bodies, there is an assumption that muscle means more power. Fans see Mark McGwire and they assume he his hitting all these home runs because of his massive upper body. But what they don't see is how fluid and tension-free McGwire's swing is. If they looked closely, they would see McGwire's top hand come off the bat and they would see magnificent lead-arm extension. That is where his power comes from. You should also take note of how tension-free his swing is through the zone. That creates bat speed and, ultimately, power.

If I were to pick a poster boy for the most fluid swing in the majors, I'd have to pick Tony Fernandez. In fact, his swing looks so effortless, it's hard to imagine he can generate the power he does. But Fernandez has the ability to smoke a pitch 450 feet and has done so often. How? A fluid, tension-free swing. When Fernandez swings, it almost looks as though he were playing a game of pepper behind the batting cages with his teammates. His is a one-part, continuous swing that generates an enormous amount of bat speed.

And that is the point I'm trying to make here: If you want to hit the ball with power, you have to create bat speed. And to create bat speed, you must release all the tension in your muscles that will block or slow down your swing. Coaches, if you see a hitter grimacing or grinding his teeth, you'll know he is trying to muscle the ball. Tell him to relax. Swing easy.

Flaw No. 5: Top-hand Rollover

OK, so here's my other pet peeve: Rolling over the wrists during the swing, which is caused by top-hand dominance. My other pet peeve — back-foot hitting — is often connected to this pet peeve because most back-foot hitters rollover their wrists. The problem with this? It breaks off the swing, cuts it short. The top-hand roll over is just as much a poison to hitting as back-foot hitting because it breaks off the swing prematurely and creates all sorts of problems.

Here's a perfect example of a young hitter rolling over his wrists too soon. Notice how the body is jerked away from the hitting area.

Now look at this swing with its great extension and flat hands. This virtually is the perfect swing. Quite a difference from the wrist-rollover swing, right?

Remember to always keep that top hand underneath.

The most obvious problem with top-hand rollover is that it creates topspin on the ball. And remember, topspin is a no-no. Topspin brings the ball back to earth more quickly, which is why in the Lau system, we're shooting for backspin. We want distance. We want the ball to travel.

Hitters who use top-hand rollover are the classic two-part swingers. As they start their swing, the bat enters the zone flat. But as they roll their wrists over, the swing veers off its flat course as the bat is jerked over. This is the second part of the swing. One reason this is bad news is the before-mentioned topspin. Another unwanted consequence is that the hitter tends to lose his leverage because the wrists, by turning over, are actually pulled back closer to his body. It is almost impossible then to drive the ball to the opposite field and the hitter is limited in where he can hit the ball and what pitches he can hit. Trying to hit an outside pitch with top-hand rollover results in a lot of harmless grounders to the shortstop (if you're a right-handed hitter), those grounders topspinning along.

Even today you can witness a fair share of top-hand rollover hitters in the major leagues. And some have had fabulous careers, players such as Paul Molitor and Cal Ripken Jr. But these players very rarely were able to hit with authority to the opposite field. And to be honest, their success has hinged predominantly on their superior athletic ability, not their technique.

See the ball, hit the ball. George Brett knew how to do it.

Chapter 8:

The Brain: It Can Help and Hurt Your Hitting

Ever notice when you get into a slump in any athletic endeavor the amount of people that are eager to help you? Fall into a one-for-25 slide in baseball and it seems everyone has a solution for you, from your teammates to your coach to your family. Your head is pulling out. Your stance is all wrong. Your bat is too heavy. You name it: Everyone's identified the problem. The problem is, of course, that you can do more damage and prolong your slump by taking too much advice. Listening to everyone's suggestions often only clogs the mind. This is when the brain can get in the way of hitting. If the brain is trying to process too much information, the message it finally sends to the body is slowed. And hitting is all about timing and quick reactions. You want that message from the brain to the body to occur instantly. The point is this: When mired in a slump, be wary of taking in too much advice. Don't create an information overload.

Hey, the truth is, everyone goes into a slump. Everyone. Even the great hitters. In baseball, as with any other sport, you have to accept a certain degree of failure. As you've probably heard a million times, the best hitters in the game, the .300 hitters, fail seven out of 10 times. What keeps a great hitter great is his ability to fight through slumps. As I've pointed out before, there often is a mechanical reason for why a hitter isn't hitting well. Maybe he's not starting his swing soon enough. Maybe his top hand has become too dominant. But sometimes slumps occur simply because of your mental approach. You can't be successful at anything unless you first believe you can be successful. Yes, I believe in mind over matter. Your brain can do wonderful things if you let it and convince it to.

Mental Approach: Tunnel Vision is Good

One way to assure self-confidence is to always go to the plate with a plan. Have an idea what you're going to try and accomplish in each particular at-bat. Are you going try to move the runner from second to third? Are you trying to lift a fly ball to score a runner from third? Focus on your plan. All the hours of batting practice and perfecting your swing are now behind you. It's just you and the pitcher. And know that pitcher. Do your homework. Know your enemy. Have all that information and data processed before you step to the plate. Once you get to the plate, clear your mind of any unnecessary thoughts and simply focus on the plan. Sometimes you can avoid slumps or pull yourself out of a slump just by returning to the basics. Wipe out the past and concentrate on the present, this at-bat. Forget about the past failures and tell yourself that you will come through in this at-bat. You're better than the pitcher. Show him.

An excellent way to maintain that focus and block out all possible distractions is to use what I call the tunnel-vision technique. Envision a tunnel between the pitcher's delivery point and the hitting zone. Mentally block out everything else around it. Your mind now will direct all its attention toward this tunnel. Track the ball in this tunnel. Prepare yourself to hit the ball when the pitcher's lead leg touches down and the ball emerges from the tunnel and approaches you. Tunnel vision. The great thing about this approach is it not only eliminates all unwanted distractions, it can also improve your selectiveness regarding which pitches to hit. If you can envision a tunnel that ends right at the strike zone, you probably won't swing at many bad pitches because you've trained your mind not to respond to anything outside that tunnel. Any pitch that drifts out of the tunnel is ignored. Tunnel vision is a great tool to train your mind to concentrate on the task at hand.

So, have a plan before each at-bat. And benefit from tunnel vision. Many slumps occur because hitters lose their focus or get distracted. That's where the expression "beating yourself" comes from. Believe me, there are enough people wanting you to fail (namely your opponents). Don't give them any help.

A Little Cockiness is OK

Sports is as much a battle of egos as it is a battle of physical ability. I've always believed that. A big ego doesn't gurantee you'll perform better than your opponent but understand this: Lack of confidence and self-doubt will beat you every time. If you think the pitcher is better than you, you have virtually no shot at getting a hit.

That's why a little cockiness and swagger isn't such a bad thing. Feeling good about yourself often translates into peforming well. Of course, don't go overboard. Overconfidence can beat you just as easily as having no confidence. Just tell yourself: Hey, the pitcher's good, but he's not *that* good.

Seize the Moment

Some hitters and some hitting instructors adhere to one of the most befuddling philosophies in baseball: Take that first pitch. I've never understood that thinking. Why take a pitch when it's possible that the pitch might be the best pitch you'll see all week? This is an absolutely silly mental approach that can, without a doubt, contribute to slumps. If you're a serious baseball fan, you've probably noticed that Wade Boggs always took that first strike. In other words, unless the pitcher is incredibly wild, Boggs started many at-bats behind in the count and at a disadvantage. Once again, this is a baseball philosophy that complicates hitting rather than simplifies it. It's a little bit analogous to starting with a crazy launch position. Yes, some hitters can start in a crazy launch position and then get their bat back to the proper launch position and still be successful. And yes, Boggs has delivered over 3,000 hits and enjoyed a very successful hitting career in the big leagues. But just think for a minute about how many great pitches Boggs has let go by. How many more hits could he have produced had he been more aggressive?

I prefer to preach aggressiveness at the plate. If you see a strike, if you see a pitch in your tunnel, go after it. Attack. Attack. Attack. Let me give you an example: How would you like it if suddenly the rules of the game were changed and hitters had to start each at-bat down one strike in the count? How many hitters do you think would favor that rule change? Hitters would be furious. But that is essentially what you're doing if your mental aproach consists of taking that first strike. Being behind in the count, in essence, forfeits some of your power over to the pitcher. Being behind in the count makes you a defensive hitter. Bottom line? If you see a good pitch, hit it.

Two Kinds of Slumps

There is more than one kind of slump that hitters endure. Some slumps are simply numbers slumps. Sometimes you can be drilling the ball almost every at-bat and have no hits to show for it. Sometimes you can have games in which you hit four line drives and each one happens to be right at a fielder. The next day, you're 0-for-4 in the box score. Does that mean you've started a slump? Of course not. In reality, you're actually in a hitting groove. The tricky part, however, is convincing yourself to ignore the numbers. That's where trust comes in. If you believe in yourself and trust yourself, you will continue with the same mental approach even though the results aren't rewarding. Some hitters, though, can get swayed into believing they need to start making adjustments because those line drives didn't translate into hits. If you hit a line drive, you can claim victory no matter if it's an out or a hit. Hitting a line drive or hitting a ball squarely is your goal. Don't confuse achieving your goals with achieving a particular batting average all the time. Those line drives eventually will find a hole. Don't worry.

The other kind of slump, naturally, is an 0-for-20 type characterized by weak groundouts and pop-ups. Typically, in this kind of slump, your mechanics are out of whack. Your swing is messed up. You're chasing bad balls. Your mental approach is poor. By the time you're 0-for-20, you're suddenly believing you're never going to get another hit. OK, now you're in a *real* slump that you need to address. Just know the difference.

Success Can Breed Slumps

Believe it or not, sometimes hitters fall into slumps because of success. What happens in this scenario is the hitter becomes so confident in his hitting ability – he may be raking every pitch thrown at him – that he suddenly believes he is invincible. The hitter then starts swinging at balls out of the strike zone. And it doesn't take much imagination to figure out what happens next. Once a hitter starts swinging at balls out of the strike zone, his swing starts to fall apart. This is the type of slump that a hitting instructor should be able to spot quickly. And fix quickly. Be aggressive at the plate and be confident. But be selective. Swing at strikes. Remember: You can't put a good swing on a bad pitch.

Be Wary of Too Much Advice

As I mentioned before, often times when you fall into a slump, you will start getting advice from every direction. Your hitting coach. Your teammates. Your relatives. Everyone suddenly has the answer. Well, the truth is, no, they don't. Take advice only from those you trust, which, in theory, should be a short list starting with your hitting instructor. And hitting instructors, as I've warned before, don't obsess or nitpick your hitters during slumps. Look for simple solutions. Don't overload the hitter with so much data to process that he starts to think too much during a slump about his mechanics. Quite often there are easy mechanical answers, such as starting the swing sooner. Or being more selective (swinging at strikes). And hitters should look within themselves for simple solutions, too. Block out all the ridiculous advice you may get from uninformed sources. Trust in yourself and your hitting instructor. The two of you should know the subject matter. So just identify the problem, mental or mechanical, and seek the simplest solution.

Slump Busters

Once you've identified the problem, you're going to need help from your brain to break out of a slump. You're going to have to convince yourself mentally that you can succeed again. What I tell students and my hitters is that they need to accept a certain amount of failure. During the course of a season, failure is inevitable. So go easy on yourself. Accept some failure. After all, seasons are long affairs. They are marathons, not sprints. In the major leagues, you will get close to 650 at-bats per season. During that span, you will slump. If you've convinced yourself of that reality, you've got a much better chance of breaking free from slumps. Accepting some degree of failure is step No. 1.

Baby Steps

Step No. 2 may appear like something right out of a self-help book, but it has merit in baseball: Take baby steps. What I mean by that is when you're trying to break out of slumps, seek small rewards at the beginning. Go into a game with a modest goal such as "Today, I want to hit one ball right on the screws. If I can do that, I'm going to be happy and sleep well." After a few games, you may tell yourself that you want to hit two balls hard. What this does is promote confidence. Slowly, as you continue to reach your modest goals each night, you begin to believe in yourself again. You are basically training your brain to think positively again. Instead of the negative thoughts that most likely were inherent during your slump, you begin to think you're capable of succeeding again.

Another element to remember about slumps is that as painful as they are to endure, they do make you stronger. The adage that what doesn't kill you makes you stronger is true. Being able to fight through slumps makes you a better overall hitter. It matures you. It prepares you for future potholes, future slumps. Once you get through one slump, you can always tell yourself you can get through another.

Situational Hitting

We now turn to the other aspect of a hitter's mental approach to the game: Situational hitting. Not all of hitting calls for line drives to the gaps or three-run homers, though, as a hitter, you certainly wouldn't turn those down. But some situations in baseball call for a different mental approach depending on where the runners are on base and how many outs there are. There are situations when grounding out to the second baseman is certainly OK, especially if it advances a runner from second to third and there are still less than two outs.

The two most common forms of situational hitting come up when there is a runner on second base with no one out, and when there is a runner on third and less than two outs. In the first situation, naturally the hitter wants to get that runner to third any way he can so the next hitter can possibly drive the runner in with simply a fly out. Does that mean the hitter should purposely swing weakly? No, because a base hit will not only get that runner to third, but it could also score him. But what we don't want is a two-hopper to the third baseman or a routine grounder to deep short that doesn't move the runner off second base. That is a wasted at-bat. And that is called losing baseball. It is also selfish baseball and you see a lot more of it in baseball today than you did years ago.

So how does the hitter get himself in the proper mental approach to advance the runner from second to third? Use that tunnel-vision approach we have discussed previously. You're looking for a pitch in a specific location – on the outer half of the plate. You want a pitch there because you're going to atttempt to drive the ball in a direction that will allow the runner to advance. That direction should be anywhere from the left of where the shortstop is positioned, not necessarily just to the right of second base, as you probably were taught at an early age. If you hit a ground ball to the left of the shortstop, the runner on second should still be able to advance. And don't necessarily assume you have to have a ground ball. If you put a good swing on the ball and drive it to the outfield in our specified direction, the runner still should be able to tag up and advance. You're still accomplishing your mission even with a fly out.

Back Off the Plate

What should you do mechanically to drive the ball toward this specified area? Naturally, you'll want to release your bat slighty later than normal (delay your start) to avoid pulling the ball. But you also need to take into account the pitcher's motives at this point. The pitcher obviously is going to make your objective challenging by trying to pitch you inside. He will likely pound you pitch after pitch inside. How do you combat his tactics? Simply back off the plate with your stance. A few inches should suffice. This should give you the room you need to direct those inside pitches toward the specified area.

Getting That Runner Home

The other most common type of situational hitting occurs when there is a runner on third and less than two outs. Chances are, in a tight game, the infield is drawn in, hoping to make a play at the plate on any ground ball. As a hitter, you're now being called upon to drive a fly ball deep enough to allow the runner to tag up at third and score. To me, the best place to drive a fly ball is from left-center field to the right-field line. Once again, you'll want to release the bat a little later so you direct the ball to the specified area. You're also going to want to hit slightly under the ball so you achieve some altitude, but not so dramatically that you collapse your swing. Just a slight uppercut. You're aiming to hit the ball somewhere between about 4 o'clock and 8 o'clock on the "watch dial" of the baseball. Hitting the ball there will provide the necessary altitude you need to get that ball to the outfield deep enough to accomplish the mission.

Why Would Anyone Switch Hit?

I want to close this chapter on the mental approach to hitting with a discussion on the theory of switch-hitting. The longer I've been around baseball and the more I have studied the concepts of hitting, the more I have questioned the basic theory behind switch-hitting. In fact, I have reached the point where I don't see the value of switch-hitting at all.

Think about this: Every switch-hitter who has ever played the game always has had a stronger, natural side of the plate from which he hits. Why would anyone purposely waste any at-bats from their weaker side? Yes, yes, I know all the old school theories on the value of switch-hitting: It is always better to have a breaking ball come toward you than move away from you, for vision purposes. And yes, it has been believed for years that it is far better to have right-handed hitters match up against left-handed pitchers (at least for offensive strategy) and vice versa. But the game is changing. And it *has* changed, thanks to the Lau System of Hitting. Statistics will bear out that hitters using the Lau method can hit right-handed or left-handed pitchers equally as well. This not only eliminates that whole righty vs.

lefty maneuvering that managers love to overmanage with late in games, it elimi-nates the very premise of switch-hitting.

Let me explain it another way: The reason switch-hitting really became popular in the '40s, '50s, and '60s was because the primary school of hitting was the pull school of hitting, the Ted Williams pull school of hitting. Almost every hitter in the game was taught to be a dead-pull hitter. Of course, it's a little tough to be terribly successful as a pull hitter against intelligent pitchers who are running curve balls away from you. As we have explained previously, when a pull hitter attempts to hit a curve ball away from him, the result is usually a weak ground ball. This is why switch-hitting rose in popularity. The dead-pull hitters found they could be more successful if they always had that curve ball coming toward them rather than mov-ing away. So they switched sides of the plate. And even by hitting with their "weak-er" side of the plate, they improved their overall average slightly. But we no longer are shackled by just one school of hitting. We no longer are restricted by dead pull hitting. In the Lau System of Hitting, hitters can cover the entire plate no matter in what direction the pitch is heading.

To further illustrate my point, let me ask you this: Who was the last switch-hitter to flirt with hitting.400? Yet George Brett has. Larry Walker has. Tony Gwynn has. None of these great hitters are switch-hitters. And all three use the Lau System of Hitting. It makes little difference to any of those hitters whether they are facing a lefty or a righty because they have or had the ability to cover the entire plate. Here's a more recent example. Chipper Jones, one of the more well-known switch-hitters today, is far better from his dominant side, his left side. From the left side in 1997, Jones hit 20 home runs with 90 RBIs. From the right side, he hit one home run and had 21 RBIs. In 1998, he hit 32 homers with 89 RBIs from the left side. From the right side, he hit two homers with 18 RBIs. So why does he continue to switch hit? Only he can tell you. Another example is Royals Rookie of the Year Carlos Beltran, who in 1999 hit.300 with 15 home runs and 88 RBIs from his dominant left side, but hit only.265 with two home runs and 20 RBIs from his right side. Granted, both of these players had far more at-bats from the left side because there are more right-handers to face. But even doubling their output from the right side wouldn't justify the switch-hitting approach.

It seems to me that switch-hitting is yet another old school philosophy that needs to be put on a shelf, right next to back-foot hitting and rolling the wrists over.

Chapter 9:

Today's Best Hitters and Why They're the Best

In this chapter we'll examine the best hitters in baseball and break down each hitter's swing and the qualities that make him exceptional. If you're going to emulate major league hitters, and normally I don't advocate that, this nonetheless would be an excellent list from which to start.

Larry Walker

The thing I love about Larry Walker is that he has an exceptionally balanced stance. And he starts his bat in the launch position (no wasted steps or motions during the swing). Notice his head, too, which is always in a perfect position to track the ball. While Walker seemingly likes to pull the ball to hit his home runs, he still has the ability to cover the plate and drive the ball to left-center field. He has good lead-arm extension. Mostly, Walker keeps both hands on the bat. But he doesn't roll his wrists over. And even on occassion he does release that top hand. His hands stay really flat through the course of the swing. It is a beautiful one-piece swing.

Another admirable part of Walker's swing is his hip rotation. Excellent weight transfer. All of his stored energy explodes into the ball at the point of contact. Don't be fooled into thinking that all of his glowing statistics are a result of his playing at Coors Field. He posted some superb numbers at Montreal, too. Walker incorporates all of Lau's Laws, especially starting with his stance and his launch position. And while he doesn't always take his top hand off the bat, he doesn't have to because he is able to keep his hands flat during the swing. You don't always have to take that top hand off if you can keep your hands flat anyway and get the proper lead-arm extension.

Larry Walker

Mark McGwire

One of the first things I noticed about McGwire when he broke into the league was he was basically a "hooker." He hooked or pulled everything. He couldn't hit a ball to center field. Because of his swing and because he hit against his front leg, his hitting area was from left-center field to the left-field foul pole. That was it.

Then all of a sudden, within the last four years, he changed his hitting philosophy. He began to adopt many of Lau's Laws. He began to take that top hand off the bat. He began getting incredible lead-arm extension. He began pulling the knob more to get the bat to the ball. These changes led him away from being just a pull hitter who predominantly hit balls with topspin. Using many of Lau's Laws, he began to get backspin on the ball. Balls began to travel farther.

McGwire also started to get that weight off the back side. He began to get better hip rotation. He's also changed where he hits the baseball: Instead of being a 3 o'clock hitter, hitting the ball at 3 o'clock on the watch dial of the ball, to a 5 to 9 o'clock hitter. That's staying "inside" the ball as opposed to hooking around the ball. This has allowed him to deliver the ball to center field and right field. That change has been most noticeable in St. Louis. How many times have you seen on ESPN fans jumping onto the vacated flower drop behind the center-field fence in St. Louis to get a McGwire home run ball? Quite often.

The thing that impresses me the most about McGwire's change in approach is not necessarily his jump in home runs, but his jump in batting average. He had been a hitter who struggled to hit .250. Now he's consistently in the .300 range.

Mark McGwire

Sammy Sosa

When I first saw Sammy Sosa, I was working in the White Sox organization. He had his hands held really high in his stance. He had no discipline at the plate and swung at a lot of bad balls. He's not a tall guy but he is very strong, and it was this athletic strength that probably kept him in the major leagues even when he was struggling. Scouts fell in love with his raw talent. Finally, with the Cubs, he began to mature into a complete hitter.

Early on his career, the word on Sammy was that if you wanted to get him out, you simply had to throw an off-speed pitch or a curve ball. But during his maturation process and as he began to see more breaking balls and off-speed pitches, he began to make adjustments. He "quieted" his head and kept his eyes down, peering at the ball during the point of impact. He also flattened his hands during the swing and began getting better lead-arm extension. All of this allowed him to become more of a weapon at the plate because he started to hit the ball to right-center and right field. Many of his home runs are delivered to the opposite field, the sign of a hitter using flat hands. No, he doesn't always take that top hand off the bat. But he obeys many of Lau's Laws, primarily he doesn't have top-hand dominance. Even when he keeps two hands on the bat, he doesn't roll over his wrists prematurely.

Sammy Sosa provides a great example that you don't have to be 6-foot-5 and weigh 240 pounds to be a dominating power hitter. Sosa is under 6 feet tall and under 200 pounds, yet he was there, neck and neck, with McGwire in the home run races of 1998 and 1999.

Just one more interesting aspect about Sosa: Notice how he gets his weight back. Sosa picks up his lead leg and steps it back, which shifts his weight back prior to launching the swing. That weight, now stored on his back side, is then transferred to the front side as he makes his stride. This is an example of one personalized way to get that weight back, which is vital for rotation and weight transfer (sort of like the first step in the crossover drill).

Sammy Sosa

Ken Griffey Jr.

The first thing I noticed about Junior, and the first thing most people notice about Junior, is how fluid he is. And one of the reasons he looks so fluid during the course of his swing is that he keeps his hands flat so long. That's what you notice the most when you study tape and pictures of his swing. His top hand is completely underneath the bat when he is at full extension, which further illustrates the point that you don't have to take the top hand off the bat as long as you can keep your hands flat during the swing.

Now, we should also point out that Junior is one of those rare talents to come along in sports. He is like the Michael Jordan of baseball (well, a Jordan who could actually play baseball). But Junior isn't the most dedicated hitter. He's one of those guys who through ability alone is able to roll out of bed, sick as a dog, and smack three home runs that day. The rest of us can't do that. He's not a guy who works hard at the gym or studies hours of video type. He is just a natural.

The other thing I worry about Junior is his ego during the so-called "Battle in Seattle," which was the battle of egos between Alex Rodriguez and Junior (when Junior was still in Seattle). This was a battle of which player "owned" Seattle. I noticed when Rodriguez began hitting home runs a lot of times and was maybe on Junior's tail in the home run race, Junior began trying to pull everything to get further ahead. When Junior is hitting well, he is hitting home runs to all parts of the park. But when he felt intimidated, he lost his concentration a bit, simply because of his competitive nature.

Having said that, we still must marvel at Junior's talent and his swing. He starts straight up in a launch position and he has excellent balance. His hip rotation is phenomenal, giving him great weight transfer. In many cases, you can even see his back foot come off the ground as this weight transfer takes place. The result is incredible bat-head speed. And he does all of this is so gracefully. Part of that gracefulness derives from tremendous confidence. Nothing seems to bother him. When we discussed how some hitters are unable to control their brain during slumps, Junior would not be an example. He brims with self-confidence, and that is a good thing.

Ken Griffey Jr.

Alex Rodriguez

Of course, this hitter is someone very special to me because I was very much a part of his maturation process. I met him during his high school days in Miami and I remember him having to sneak away from his high school coach to get instruction from me: His high school coach didn't think he needed any instruction because Rodriguez was so physically gifted. But the truth is, Rodriguez, early on in his baseball career, was a classic case of a hitter trying to muscle the ball. My first task with him was to try to get him to stay fluid. You will still see him today using a technique I taught him in high school: Watch him in the on-deck circle taking smooth, three-quarter speed swings. I taught him that technique to get him to think about being fluid during the swing.

Rodriguez always was very eager to learn. He always was the first hitter in the cage and the last to leave. He constantly asked questions. A dream student. He stayed under my instruction until about 1997 when we finally went our separate ways. But I still believe this: If he had stayed with me, he'd be a threat to hit .400 right now with 50 homers a year.

Don't get me wrong. Alex is still a fantastic hitter. A tremendous force and weapon at the plate. And the reason is he has unbelievable power to the opposite field. He gets that power through perhaps the best lead-arm extension in the game. It looks so effortless, too. He adheres to all of Lau's Laws and really is my poster child.

I remember back in 1996 we were having dinner in Seattle on a June night. I happened to tell him that night that one day he was going to win a batting title. Well, he won it that season with a .358 average. I didn't quite think it would happen that fast but neither one of us complained. Here's the other great thing about Alex: The very next spring he called me and asked me how we were going to start polishing up his swing. He is a tireless worker.

Alex Rodriguez

Barry Bonds

Bonds is more of a rotational hitter than the other hitters in this chapter. If there is such a thing as a pure rotational-type hitter, Barry Bonds is it. For the majority of his at-bats, he is a pull hitter. But every once in a while, he exhibits better weight transfer with that rotation, which allows him to stay inside the ball (hit it between 6 and 9 o'clock because he is a left-handed hitter) and drive it to the opposite field. I think, though, if Bonds were a little less pull conscious, he could hit just as many home runs to the opposite field as he does to right field.

Somewhat like Junior, Bonds is a very confident hitter. He has a surplus of natural ability and combined with his self-confidence, he is able to break free from any prolonged slumps. He is one of those hitters who believes he is going to come through in any situation. And as we discussed in the chapter about the mental approach to the game, that is more than half the battle.

But don't be fooled into thinking that Bonds gets by on skill alone. He does obey some of Lau's Laws. One time Tony Gwynn shared a conversation he had with Bonds about how Bonds could possibly get bat speed by choking up on the bat so much. Bonds told Gwynn that he accomplished this by pulling the knob of the bat to the ball.

Barry Bonds

Manny Ramirez

Probably one of my favorite guys to watch. He is an animal at the plate. Probably one of the most aggressive hitters in the game. He attacks the hitting zone as much as any hitter in the game. If I were a pitcher, this guy would scare the you-know-what out of me. He kicks his leg up and back to get his weight back, and he comes through with unbelievable lead-arm extension. He hits the ball with power to the opposite field as well as any hitter in the game.

One time I was talking to the scouting director for Cleveland and he told me that the organization had a policy that no one was allowed to alter Manny's swing. I agreed. It is that good of a swing. If anyone did try to mess with Manny's swing, they should have their head examined. While they're looking for a new line of work, of course.

Manny, because he keeps his hands so flat through the swing and gets such great lead-arm extension, is a threat to smash any pitch in the strike zone. He has no weak spots for a pitcher to exploit. Simply one of my favorites to watch.

Manny Ramirez

Juan Gonzalez

"Juan Gone," as he is called, is an exception to one of the rules on hitting. Gonzalez is one of those rare hitters who can put a good swing on a bad pitch. He is rare. But he can do it. He hits so many balls out of the strike zone for home runs that he defies logic. He is a Lau Law-breaker in other aspects, too. For example, he does have a crazy starting position with his bat as well. But he gets away with it, and is able to get his bat back to the proper launch position in time. Well, most of the time. But I give credit where credit is due. I just don't suggest that any of you try to emulate many of the things Juan Gone does.

Yet while he does break some of the Lau Laws, he obeys many of the key ones. He gets tremendous lead-arm extension. He takes the top hand off the bat. He gets excellent rotation and weight transfer off the back side. And like Sosa, he's also interesting for his trigger (the lead leg coming back to get that weight on the back side). Unlike Sosa, he has yet another trigger for his upper body. His second trigger is the crazy starting position that gets his upper-body weight back to the launch position. He's the only hitter I can think of that is a two-trigger hitter.

Yes, Juan Gone is a fascinating hitter to watch. But there also are problems that I'm not sure even he's aware of. When he goes into slumps, I'm not sure he realizes that it may be because he's not giving himself enough time due to the crazy starting position of the bat. But this guy is an RBI machine. When there's a runner on second and two outs, Gonzalez always finds a way to get that runner in. He's possessed in that way. A great clutch hitter.

Juan Gonzalez

Rafael Palmeiro

I played Little League ball with Palmeiro. Even back then, he was fluid and smooth with his swing. Completely tension free. He's one of those guys that because his swing is so fluid, he can generate enough bat-head speed to smack a ball 400 feet without looking like he's even trying.

But if I have one complaint about Palmeiro, it's that he's a dead-pull hitter. He gets away with it because he does get excellent lead-arm extension. He has a very good stance, with a quiet head and very pronounced rotation and weight transfer. A little like Bonds in that his power comes from that rotation and weight transfer. Palmeiro's back foot almost comes off the ground at the point of impact. He's very consistent, too.

Here's what I want you to remember about Palmeiro, though: This is a guy without a bulging muscle in his body yet he is recognized as one of the game's top homer and RBI guys. He's not one to spend hours at Gold's Gym. But Palmeiro is living proof that you can create bat speed by pulling the knob of the bat to the ball and through rotation, weight transfer and lead-arm extension. He's the last guy you would think could muscle a home run. And he doesn't. He hits home runs with a fluid, tension-free swing.

The last thing I'll say about Palmeiro is this guy was born to play baseball. Nothing much has changed about his swing or his approach since he was in eighth grade. He is the epitome of "smooth."

Rafael Palmeiro

Chipper Jones

I used Chipper Jones as an example in the previous chapter on why we should aban-don the concept of switch-hitting. Chipper is a monster hitter from the left side of the plate, his dominant side. From his right side, he has little power and doesn't hit much for average. So I'm going to refrain from any more comment about his right-handed hitting. Let's talk about Chipper from the left side.

From the left side, he's a forceful power hitter. On pitches from the middle of the plate to the outside half, he demonstrates exceptional lead-arm extension. If I have a criticism of his left-handed swing, it's that he sometimes cuts it off a little too soon on pitches inside. He doesn't stay inside the ball. I think he has the ability to hit 20 home runs to the opposite field because of that lead-arm extension on pitches from the middle to the outer half of the plate.

Chipper also has the trigger, like Sosa, with his lead foot. He steps that foot back to get his weight back. Also take notice of his game face. He's got those George Brett eyes and stares down pitchers. Fearless.

Chipper Jones

Chapter 10:

The Secret to Hitting a Home Run

Without question, hitting a home run is the single most exciting act in all of sports. Perhaps nothing makes a hitter more proud and certainly nothing pumps his ego and machismo like belting a home run. You get to make your trot around the bases with all eyes on you. In the major leagues, you're almost assured of making the ESPN or CNN highlights. But hitting a home run isn't just about body-building or pumping your forearms. It's not all about strength, as I will discuss in this chapter. As George Brett once said, "Look at me, physically. I'm not a big guy. I don't have bulging muscles. But I hit over 300 home runs in the bigs. How did that happen?" It happened through proper mechanics, of course.

Wait For the Right Pitch

I can't emphasize enough the importance of waiting for and hitting the right pitch. For example, the reason Mark McGwire hit 70 home runs in 1998 wasn't because he could suddenly bench-press 450 pounds. He could always do that. But McGwire from about 1996 on became one of the most disciplined hitters in the game. He came to realize that if a pitch wasn't in the precise location (in his particular tunnel) he would not swing at it. I've seen him take pitches that were less than an inch out of the strike zone. That is how selective he has become.

Choosing what pitch you think is best for you to hit a home run varies depending upon your size and your approach to hitting. For example, I'm a taller guy, about 6 foot 4. My suitable home run pitch is about belt-high without much attention to where the pitch crosses the plate. Other hitters prefer different locations. Barry Bonds, for example, is such a pull hitter that he prefers a pitch from the middle to the inner half of the plate and somewhat below the belt. Other hitters, such as Alex Rodriguez and Manny Ramirez, two of my favorites, are just as likely to hit a home run without pulling the ball. They can just as easily smash a home run to right-center or right field by taking a ball from the middle to the outer half of the plate and driving it into the seats.

Pull Hitters

By now you should know that I'm not crazy about hitters who can only hit home runs by pulling the ball. Pitchers can spot these types of hitters from miles away and they will pitch accordingly. They will keep the ball away. So my recommendation to you pull hitters is to get deep in the box and move up toward the plate with your stance. If you're going to need an inside pitch to pull, and the pitcher is pitching you away, you'll have to adjust to get that pitch location. You should also open your stance a little bit, which gets your hips pre-started toward the rotation you'll need to get around and hook the ball. And then wait for your pitch that's close enough to you to enable you pull. In other words, reduce your tunnel vision to that hitting zone where you need the pitch to enter.

These types of pull hitters will reduce that tunnel vision to a north-and-south zone. They've already adjusted for the east-west zone by moving up on the plate. Now, they're looking for something that will enter their tunnel vision in that narrow tunnel. If they don't get it, they will lay off that pitch. That north-south zone will likely be between their mid-thighs and their chest.

Get That Bat Head Out

The next step for pull hitters in hitting a home run is to get that bat head out quicker and through the zone. To do this, you'll have to firm up that front leg much sooner. That means, during your rotation and weight transfer, you'll have to slam on the brakes sooner, as we have discussed previously. Getting that front leg firm sooner enables your bat head to get through the zone quicker and allows you to pull the ball toward the designated area, which would be between left-center field and left field.

Get Started on Time

Of course, none of these previously mentioned techniques will matter much unless you get started on time with your stride. That is paramount. If you don't get started quickly, you won't have the reaction time necessary to get the hips rotated and therefore the barrel of the bat will be late at the point of impact, if there even is a point of impact. So get in the batter's box, be prepared and get started on time.

Bat Speed and Lead-arm Extension

You're going to have to generate bat speed to hit a home run. Just ask George Brett, Larry Walker, Alex Rodriguez and so forth. These are not huge, muscular individuals. But their power came and comes from accelerated bat speed. So be conscious of pulling the knob of the bat to the ball. Resist the temptation to muscle the ball by using top-hand dominance, which will only slow the swing down and in many cases, break the swing into two parts. There has to be a mini-explosion at the point of impact, with the velocity of your bat speed crashing into velocity of the speed from the pitched ball. The greater the two velocities, the more distance the ball will travel. Pull that knob of the bat with your lead arm.

And just like any other swing I teach, make sure you get proper lead-arm extension. With a flat-hand swing and lead-arm extension, you should be able to generate backspin, which is critical in hitting a home run. Remember, back-spin balls travel further than top-spin balls.

The Watch Dial of the Ball

So where should you be aiming at the ball as you swing? Obviously, a line drive or a ground ball isn't going to help you if you're trying to knock one out of the park. So you should be concentrating on the bottom half of the ball. On the watch dial of the ball, you should be keying on space between three o'clock and nine o'clock. And if you're trying to pull a home run, you should be looking at somewhere near seven o'clock. This will get you under the ball slightly and with the proper backspin, generate the needed altitude.

Lift That Swing

OK, yes, you're gong to have to loft your swing slightly. And believe me, this is a dangerous bit of advice because the minute you start trying to hit home runs you open yourself up to the possibility of ruining your swing. Even some of the best home run hitters, such as Ken Griffey Jr. and Manny Ramirez, shake their heads at you if you suggest that they *try* to hit home runs all the time. They don't. But some situations call for the home run, and therefore there are mechanical techniques that will increase your chances of accomplishing this. One is to slightly loft your swing. In other words, swing up slightly. Not much, but enough to ensure that you're getting under the ball and creating some altitude. I can't emphasize enough how dangerous this practice can be. But as soon as the situation doesn't call for a home run, remember to return to your normal, level swing through the zone.

For the purposes of hitting a home run, though, you will need to loft that swing. That means you will drop the bat barrel slightly, about one-quarter of the way through the swing. You don't want to drag the bat through the swing, like a slow-pitch softball player would. But drop the bat barrel slightly to create a lofty swing.

Don't Ignore Lau's Laws

Having said all this, you can still be a potent home run hitter by using all of Lau's Laws. Manny Ramirez, Juan Gonzalez and Alex Rodriguez are all perfect examples of hitters who don't necessarily have to abandon Lau's Laws and become dead-pull hitters just to hit a home run. These hitters, when they look to hit home runs in certain situations, stick mainly to their principles and are able to drive a ball to either gap or even to right field to accomplish the mission. They may loft their swing slightly, but they maintain their discipline in accordance with all of the other Lau's Laws. And if you become successful through my teachings, you will be able to hit home runs with minor adjustments as well.

Summing It Up

Here are the points to remember if you're trying to hit a home run, especially if you're trying to do so by pulling the ball:

- Wait for the right pitch. Be selective. Be aggressive, but only go after those pitches in your particular tunnel.

- Move up toward the plate which will counteract the pitcher's strategy to pitch you away.

- Get that front leg firmed up quicker, which allows the bat head to get through the zone faster.

- Make sure to get your stride started on time. You can't be late because you need all the reaction time you can get.

- Remember bat speed. You need accelerated bat speed so concentrate on pulling the knob of the bat toward the ball and avoid trying to muscle the ball, which will cause top-hand dominance.

• You need altitude on the ball, so you're going to try to aim toward the 3 o'clock to 9 o'clock area on the watch dial of the ball. With flat hands and proper lead-arm extension, this will enable you to get backspin, and that, in turn, will give you the distance you need.

• Loft the swing slightly. Drop the barrel of the bat slightly as you get about one-quarter into your swing. You want the ball to elevate, so you need to lift the ball.

Chapter 11:
The Best Way to Hit in Fast-pitch Softball

Women's fast-pitch softball is rapidly increasing in popularity at the high school and college level. As it gains popularity and attendance increases, more scholarships are being handed out in this program. But there is one problem with this sport. A major one.

There isn't enough offensive production. Games are dominated by pitchers and scores are often 2-1 or 1-0, reminiscent of World Cup soccer games. It doesn't have to be that way.

The primary reason that pitchers dominate in fast-pitch softball is poor technique among the hitters. And poor instruction from the coaches. I will argue that the same philosophy in my system of hitting, the same Lau's Laws, apply to fast-pitch softball. There is no reason why women cannot hit in fast-pitch softball with the power and authority that men do in baseball. If coaches would listen, I believe that Lau's Laws could revolutionize the state of fast-pitch softball.

Notice how the hips are opening prematurely as her bat is starting to get "around" the ball, a process that develops a long swing.

What is the Problem?

In every fast-pitch softball game I've observed, I've noticed the same thing with hitters. They stride as they swing. Therefore they very rarely hit the ball to the opposite field. They also tend to try to swing faster to catch up to the ball, rather than start their stride sooner. In other words, their mechanics are wrong from the get-go. At some point they are taught that the stride and the swing are one in the same, rather than the baseball approach which is to stride first and then swing. I'm not sure why hitters are taught this in fast-pitch softball. The difference between softball and baseball are not that dramatic. True, the delivery from the pitcher in softball comes underneath. And true, the pitcher in softball is standing about 10 feet closer. But the challenge facing the hitter in each sport is the same. The ball is coming at a rapid speed and the hitter needs to be prepared to attack the ball in the best manner possible.

The other major problem I've noticed is that these softball hitters are top-hand dominant. In other words, they have the classic two-part swings and break off the swing as they roll their wrists over. And you know what this causes: dead-pull hitting and a lot of weak ground balls. Go observe a fast-pitch softball game if you don't believe and just count the number of weak ground balls that are hit. That is the result of top-hand dominance. Now, I've heard coaches argue that is because the trajectory of the pitched ball is different than it is in baseball (the ball tends to rise because of the underhand delivery). But the point they're missing is that the ball rising is actually an advantage for the hitter. With the Lau Laws, it will be even easier to create backspin because of the ball's trajectory. Hitters won't have to focus so hard at hitting between 6 o'clock at 9 o'clock because at the last split second, the ball will possibly jump up into that watch-dial position. Hey, that's perfect if you're trying to hit backspin.

Solution No. 1

For some reason, and I seriously don't know why, softball hitters and instructors haven't figured out that you need reaction time to hit the softball. The easiest way to accomplish this is to start sooner. Start your stride sooner. This gives you reaction time, which is precious, especially if you believe you actually have less reaction time in fast-pitch softball. Give yourself that extra time by starting sooner.

In baseball, I tell hitters to start their stride when the pitcher's front leg hits the ground. Just to be safe, just to get softball hitters started in time, I would recommend that softball hitters start when they see the pitcher's hand reach their hip. That's before their lead leg hits the ground.

Now, I can already hear some softball hitting instructors starting to protest. They'll argue that if you start the stride that early, the hitter will be vulnerable to the change-up, which is a pitcher's valuable weapon in fast-pitch softball. But I'll argue right back that the reason the off-speed pitch has become so effective in fast-pitch softball is that hitters are taught to stride and swing at the same time. Since their hands are already moving with their stride, of course they're going to be unable to stop and make adjustments in time to hit a change-up. But remember, in baseball, in my teachings, the hands are the last to release. The stride starts with the hands and weight still back. So if the change-up comes, the hands are still back far enough to make an adjustment and hit the off-speed pitch squarely.

Note the dominant top hand pushing through the swing.

And here's the wrist rollover. And look where the ball is headed — down. Another top-spin grounder.

There is still too much weight on the back foot here. Notice how the hitter's back leg is flexing, which tells you it is supporting weight.

Solution No. 2

The same principles apply from Lau's Laws. Pull the bat knob toward the ball, making sure you're not dominating with the top hand. This will create bat speed. Now you have the potential to hit with some power and authority. Don't believe me? Go try it. And remember, fast-pitch softball hitters, you have one huge advantage over your counterparts in baseball: the size of the softball. You've got a target that is at least twice the size of a baseball. This doubles your chances of hitting the ball squarely. And another thing: Because the softball is bigger, it has much larger seams. That means with the proper backspin, the ball will fight the laws of gravity with much more force because those larger seams are cutting through the air resistance with more force.

There's no reason for all the weak ground balls and soft flares that you witness in softball. If players started capitilizing on using backspin, you might see a revolution in the game. If one player tried it, that player might become the Hank Aaron of softball.

Of course, you'll also have to adhere to the other Lau Laws to ensure backspin. Hit toward the watch dial (6 o'clock to 9 o'clock for right-handed hitters), keep your hands flat, and concentrate on your follow-through with proper lead-arm extension.

The Major Stumbling Block

The top-hand dominance is the major culprit is prohibiting softball from becoming an offense-oriented game. Yes, I'm purposely being redundant to drive home a point. I have yet to see a fast-pitch softball hitter exhibit any lead-arm extension, and I've yet to see any fast-pitch softball hitter demonstrate flat hands through the swing. Watching fast-pitch softball today is a bit like watching the back-foot, wrist roll-over hitters in baseball from the '40s, '50s and '60s. They are all pull conscious with blatant two-part swings. That's why, in my mind, you see such a pitcher-dominated game in fast-pitch softball. Hitters are getting themselves out. Look at it this way: Not all of these pitchers are the softball equivalent of Nolan Ryan. They're not throwing 105 miles per hour.

Here's a much better softball swing. Notice how the front leg has firmed up, the weight is off the back side and the hands are flat.

Let Me Help

I would absolutely love to have two weeks instructing hitting on any fast-pitch softball team in the country. Seriously. And I hereby challenge any coach out there to call me on it. Bring me in and if I can't dramatically improve your team's overall hitting, I will waive the cost of the instruction. That's how strongly I feel I can alter the state of offense in fast-pitch softball and revolutionize the game. What do yo have to lose? I will gurantee improvement. And if you're not up for that challenge, simply read the chapters in this book on the drills associated with Lau's Laws and apply the techniques I have described. Tell me if there's not a distinctive improvement. I can assure there will be a drastic change in your team's overall batting average and its run production.

Chapter 12

Lau's Language

Over the last few decades, as more and more hitters adopt the Lau system of hitting, the language of hitting has changed. The way we communicate the instruction of hitting has changed dramatically as well. Tired and worn-out clichés such as "keep your front shoulder in" or "stay back when you swing" or "roll your wrists over" have slowly evaporated from the game's language. Not everywhere, mind you. Go to a Little League game or a college game or even some major league games and you'll still hear some misguided coach or batting instructor barking out those outdated instructions. But we are embarking on a new age of hitting in baseball, as evidenced by the increased offensive production. As we have mentioned before, the offensive explosion in baseball can be explained in many ways. But the principle reason is the unquestioned improvement in technique. And with that improved technique has come a change in the way we communicate the teaching of hitting.

Cause and Effect

Understand that everything you do as a hitter has ramifications. Each act you commit while swinging (the cause) produces an effect. That explains much of the language used in instructing hitting. For example, in the old school philosophy, there was a constant fear of hitters lunging at the ball. To combat this effect, instructors barked out what I now consider a rather bizarre language of instruction. Instructors would tell their hitters to hit against their front leg, or stay back as they proceeded to swing. Those are clichés you'll never hear me utter, and someday, hopefully, those are cliches that will never be uttered again in a batting cage or on a baseball diamond. As we have pointed out numerous times in this book, the danger of hitting against your front leg or staying back (keeping your weight back and squishing the bug) causes many other problems (effects), such as forcing the bat head out too soon. That creates a long swing.

The new language, the Lau Language, contains a different approach. I know my father used the term "weight shift" back in the '70s and I think the reason he used that language was in direct response to the teachings of the Ted Williams era. In that era, hitters were taught to keep all their weight planted on their back side. And I think to steer hitters away form that philosophy, my father often talked of weight shift in order to get players to rotate toward their front side.

Yet I am cautious in using the term weight shift because sometimes if you harp on that the hitter will overcompensate and his head will display too much lateral movement forward. I may instead focus on rotation of the hips and having the back foot turn toward the pitcher with the back heel pointed towards the sky. That will encourage the weight shift we need without excessive movement of the head. I've always said that you have to have a stable head as you start to go to the ball.

Communication Adjustment

The point I'm trying to make here is that as an instructor, sometimes you have to adjust your language or communication depending upon what you observe as you watch a hitter. Some of the language I use tends to be effective with all hitters, such as the notion of "hitting through the ball." But what does that mean? To me, hitting through the ball means driving through the ball with flat hands and not turning the hands over too soon. Another effective term is "finish your swing." By getting the hitter to concentrate on finishing his swing, chances are the hitter is not going to cut off his swing prematurely. You've probably also heard the term "finish high." This is another piece of language or communication that should get the hitter to hit through the ball and not cut off the swing. It is physically impossible to finish your swing high (Mark McGwire style) and roll your wrists over, which would be a no-no. Of course, you need to use caution when telling a hitter to finish high, too. If the hitter gets too obsessed with finishing high he may start to elevate his swing too soon. And you can imagine the dangers of that – he won't be able to drive through the ball if he is lofting at the point of impact. So "finishing high" may not always work for everybody. Certainly, though, finishing with lead-arm extension is at the core of my teachings.

Be a hands-on teacher. It is OK to talk about "hitting through the ball" or "finishing high," but make sure the student doesn't focus too hard on one element of the swing while ignoring other elements.

The point I'm trying to make is that as an instructor, you need to recognize quickly and instinctively the problems in a swing and then adjust your language or communication accordingly. We can talk about lead-arm extension and finishing high until we're exhausted, but it won't much help a hitter if he is focusing too hard on the end of his swing and not on the point of impact. As you watch the hitter, examine the hitter's swing to determine if your language is communicating your point properly. For example, even though we preach lead-arm extension, we know that the hitter must first make contact before extending. Below is a picture of former Royals shortstop Buddy Biancalana from years ago that shows him making contact with his bat too far away from his body. Yes, he is getting extension, but he has made contact fully extended and his body isn't supporting his swing. Perhaps somebody taught him to focus too hard on extension and therefore he felt he needed to extend at the point of contact, which is improper. You make contact first and then you extend through the ball and finish your swing.

The danger of poor communication despite using the proper language. Buddy Biancalana gets the right extension, but far too soon in the swing.

Paint a Picture

The final aspect about the new Lau Language and communicating deals with imagination. As an instructor, open your mind as you analyze each individual hitter. Recognize his individuality. The language you used on a previous student may not be effective on the one standing in front of you. I like to use metaphors as I teach. I like to think of weight shift as the equivalent of a whip cracking: the body's weight starts to move back, like the cocking of a whip, then the weight shifts forward toward the point of impact. The result is a whiplash effect that unleashes all the body's stored energy into the ball.

There are many ways to preach a sermon. Make sure you treat all your students as individuals.

And when I talk about hitting on the inside of the ball, I like to imagine the face of a clock where the baseball would be. The inside would be the area between 6 and 9 o'clock. In other words, paint a picture for the hitter in whatever way feels natural to you. And show him by physically getting next to him as you make your point. Be a hands-on teacher and remember the words of Albert Einstein: sometimes imagination is more important than knowledge.

Chapter 13

The State of the Game: In My Own Words

Consider this for a moment: In the last 20 years, who has emerged as a hitting instructor who is a household name? Who has emerged as being the guru of the swing? When you see a player being interviewed, how often do you see him give credit to a hitting instructor for his success? You don't hear that anymore, quite frankly. Why? Because baseball doesn't believe in one universal method of hitting. And baseball doesn't trust anyone enough to help teach their players. It's true. That's why you see the same generic techniques being taught from generation to generation.

My father, Charley Lau, used to work with every hitter on the teams he used to instruct. When he was with the Royals, he worked with all the greats, from George Brett to Hal McRae. The reason he was hired by the Yankees was to teach the entire team how to hit. They didn't tell him that he shouldn't try to instruct Reggie Jackson just because Reggie was a power hitter and therefore should be left alone. Reggie had been the poster child for the dead-pull hitter. But he listened to my dad and listened to the techniques, and he became a better hitter.

The point I'm trying to make is the method my father taught and what I'm trying to teach can help everyone. But the problem today in baseball is that organizations already are preset in their ways. In the major leagues, you have a general manager who makes all the deals, he hires the player-development guys, spends all the owner's money and what happens is the organization basically throws a ball out on the field and says, "Hey, everybody go play." He very rarely takes responsibility for his actions. He blames other people, such as pitching coaches or batting coaches or managers. These organizations today really don't believe in teaching anymore. They don't teach players. They may see a guy with power and say "Well, he's got power, leave him alone, don't mess with his swing." It doesn't make sense to me.

No More Development

Over the last five years, you've seen a radical change in the way organizations and baseball in general conduct business. It's no longer about player development. The teams that win are the teams with the most cash. Obviously, a major part of the problem is the economics of the game. When teams like the Yankees or the Braves want to win, they simply go out and buy the best players. No one takes the time to develop players anymore, or teach these players how to play. If the player isn't already an All-Star, the big-money teams aren't interested in him. And believe me, even the All-Stars don't get much help from the organizations they sign with.

What illustrates my point even more is the fact that several players have come to me and paid me out of their own pocket just to get proper instruction. Why? Because they know they won't get that instruction from the team they're with. I get kind of a chuckle out of it because often times they'll tell me, "Charley, my hitting instructor doesn't know how to help me. Can you?" It's a shame because everybody needs help. It doesn't matter what level you're at. You need instruction and guidance.

You would think that the owners would get smart and save themselves a lot of money by hiring a good instructor to teach their players the proper way to hit. But every season you see the same organizations spend boatloads of money and come up empty at playoff time, teams like the Orioles and the Dodgers. What's really sad is that these teams, after having wasted all this money, end up firing the manger or the hitting coach, as if that was the problem. The guy they should be firing is the person who signed these players who didn't produce.

A prime example of this is a good friend of mine, Jesse Barfield, who had been the hitting coach at Seattle in 1998 and 1999. During those two seasons, the Mariners hit more home runs than any team in the history of baseball. But Jesse got fired after the 1999 season. He was the scapegoat for yet another disappointing season in Seattle. The problem, of course, was the Mariners didn't have any pitching.

Another example is Walt Hrniak, who used to be the batting coach for the White Sox and was a disciple of my father's teachings. During Walt's tenure, Frank Thomas became one of the most feared hitters in the game. But once the White Sox started to become a disappointment (because of poor management decisions), they wound up firing Walt. And you've probably noticed what has happened to Frank Thomas in recent years. Funny thing is, in 1999, Frank wound up calling Walt to seek his help. You know why? Because Frank realized that he had his best years when he had discipline in his swing. And Walt was the reason behind that discipline.

One more example: Alex Rodriguez. In his first year in the bigs, he hit.232. Then we started working together and by 1996 he hit.358 and won a batting title. That's how much difference good instruction can make. And those are just some of the rewards for a hitting instructor.

On the other hand, I probably shouldn't be complaining about baseball's ignorance because I enjoy having these players come to me. I enjoy having them solicit my help. So if baseball wants to continue ignoring the importance of proper teaching, that just means more business for me.

I really don't blame all the hitting coaches around, either. They are restrained from instructing too much. Most organizations have a hands-off policy when it comes to teaching their superstars. Hitting coaches want to teach, but many times they are not permitted to do so.

There Was a Time They Listened

Back in the early '70s, there was an organization that believed in player development — the Kansas City Royals. My father had the opportunity to teach players like George Brett and Hal McRae the proper way to hit. And what happened? Well, of course, Brett made the Hall of Fame. And just remember how many kids tried to emulate George over the years, getting in that crouched stance, weight back, peering at the pitcher. And George never hesitated to give credit to his mentor, my father.

What Makes the System So Good?

The true secret of the swing is twofold: One, you need to get lead-arm extension, and two, to need to prevent top-hand dominance or rolling over the wrist. That was what my father introduced, researched and brought out into the open. I feel that I've followed up that research with scientific proof and unveiled that proof in this book.

I'm not saying that you should simply cut your top hand off and not use it. Clearly, it serves as a guide through the swing. I'm also not saying that the top hand should come off the bat at the point of impact. Sometimes you'll see hitters reach out with a one-handed swing and loop a fly ball to the opposite field. That's not what I'm advocating. I'm only concerned with what the top hand does after the point of impact.

One of the biggest obstacles my father and I have had to overcome is the accusation from the old school philosophers that the Lau System of Hitting will reduce power in the hitter. Clearly, that is not the case. Guys like Larry Walker, Manny Ramirez, Mark McGwire serve as perfect examples for the doubters. These guys hit between 30 and 70 home runs a year.

In fact, I proved that the Lau System is the most effective manner in which to hit for power because it generates bat speed by pulling the knob of the bat to the ball. Pulling the knob of the bat to the ball rather than pushing the bat keeps the bat inside the ball and helps generate backspin. A ball with backspin scientifically will travel further than a ball with topspin.

The other old school philosophy that I believe I've torn down is the one that insists that power hitters get their power from their hips. Baloney. You get power from bat speed and bat velocity. That bat speed comes from pulling the knob of the bat to the ball and then through hip rotation and the subsequent weight transfer.

Fighting the Old-schoolers

The thing that has bothered me the most over the years is the way people have reacted to my father, who was the greatest hitting coach and teacher of all time. It was almost as if they were resentful that a guy who never hit above.255 in the big leagues could be right in his teachings. Coaches everywhere dismissed his teachings or attacked them.

These attacks really started when my father's hitters began taking their top hand off the bat after the point of impact. Coaches were adamantly against that mainly because they were reluctant to change. I'm sure this is normal for any new teachings. We often fear the unknown and we often fear change. While I have always believed that coaches should be willing to explore new ideas, not all coaches feel that way, especially the old school philosophers borne from the Ted Williams pull-hitting philosophy.

But as a coach, why shouldn't you try to do what's best for your hitters? Rather than violently attacking a new approach, why wouldn't these coaches toss out their horse-and-buggy thinking and adopt new techniques? I don't know why. It's hard to fight ignorance and it's been a long, uphill battle for three decades.

I remember talking to John Olerud one day and he shared with me a story about how he taught himself to hit. When he was young, he went out and bought a copy of my dad's book *The Art of Hitting*. He said he patterned himself after George Brett, whose pictures are displayed predominantly in that book. Anyway, Olerud went on to tell me that while he was in college at the University of Washington, he remembered a game in which he drilled a 450-foot home run to straightaway center field. He did so, of course, by taking his top hand off the bat after the point of impact and then finishing the swing with great lead-arm extension. He got back to the dugout, he said, and his coach greeted him and said, "John, for Heaven's sake, keep two hands on the bat." Olerud said he was in absolute disbelief.

But therein lies the problem. Coaching ignorance. Did that coach really expect that Olerud could have hit the ball further than 450 feet with both hands on the bat? These coaches should be ashamed of themselves.

What's really sad, though, is all the wasted opportunites caused by the old school philosophers and the coaching ignorance. Sometimes I wonder just how many more players could have gotten out of the minor leagues or had better careers if they had just had proper instruction. I'm sure the list is endless.

I came across an interesting article in 1998 that I'd like to share with you. It read: "In the church of hitting, there are many pews. But that wasn't always the case. Thirty years ago the church was ruled by the orthodoxy of two-handed extension on follow-through. Hitters were required to hold onto a bat with two hands as if it were a ladder up from hell. Then a heretic former catcher named Charley Lau proclaimed to his belief in the one-handed release. This caused much gnashing of the teeth among the orthodox. A one-handed extension would reduce power and efficiency, they warned. Now, Mark McGwire extends with one hand in the '90s. Many of the game's better hitters embrace Lau's principles. But no convert is more significant than McGwire. Should he break Roger Maris' record (he did), Lau's theory will be canonized. And McGwire's persistence in converting from a conventional two-handed extension will be rewarded."

That's powerful stuff, friends. I was tickled to read that. But it gives you an idea of the fight that was on my father's hands and now mine. This is why I wanted to do this book: to provide scientific fact and data so the people could have the evidence for themselves. I can't change everyone's mind. But if you have an open mind and are willing to learn, the answers are in these pages.

I'm not saying all coaches are idiots and all coaches are resistent. On the other hand, you simply can't convince some people. I remember having an argument with one coach who was discussing my system of hitting and he cracked, "Oh, that's that lunge system of hitting." That's yet another misconception spawned by ignorance. Some coaches believed that because you get the weight off your back side in my system of hitting that you automatically are lunging at the ball. Nonsense. In fact, just the opposite is true. You can't lunge at anything with your front leg firmed up. Just try it sometime. It doesn't work. But I knew I couldn't possibly convince this coach of the facts.

But in a way, arguments such as those helped inspire me to do this book because everytime I heard an attack or an argument against my father's teachings, I was determined to go out and provide scientific proof to disprove each of their arguments. I was determined to have plenty of ammunition each time someone disputed one of Lau's Laws.

I also decided to do this book as a tribute to the kids out there. I work with many kids at an early age and in many degrees, that teaching them is far more rewarding than teaching big leaguers. It is my hope that coaches at the Little League level will buy this book and take its information to heart. When you think about it, most Little League coaches are not baseball experts. Some are insurance salesmen or stock brokers or you name it. Wouldn't it be great for them to be equipped with the best teaching tools available? I remember a story George Brett shared at his Hall of Fame induction about his oldest son, who was playing t-ball. George had been an unofficial assistant coach to the team and had spent hours teaching his son the Lau system. Well, it seems George had to go out of town for a couple of weeks and when he got back to watch his son play, he said, "My God. What happened to your swing, son?" What happened is that in George's absence, the regular coach of the team had re-taught George's son with the old school philosophy. Yes, the battle still rages today.

That's really why I decided to write this book. I wanted to provide the information necessary for players to completely change and improve their baseball abilities, regardless of their age. All the information you need, whether you are a player or a coach, is right here in these pages.

I hope you have fun learning them and adapting them to your style of play.

Sweet Swings!

Photo Credits

SV Sports / Active Images – front cover center, 35, 37, 41, 44, 45, 48, 51, 55, 57 top right, bottom left, 59, 62, 65, 70, 73, 74, 76, 79, 81, 84, 86, 88, 90, 92, 96, 98, 99, 100, 102, 107, 111, 113, 115, 117, 119, 121, 123, 125, 127, 128, 130, 131, 133, 135, 136, 138, 139, 142, 143, 144, 145, 146, 152 right, 156, 158, 161, 175, 177, 179, 181, 183, 185, 187, 189, 191, 193, 210, 211, 212, back cover.

Charley Lau Jr. – 39, 49, 103, 104, 109, 201, 204, 206

Junior Baseball Magazine – front cover left, right, 67, 72, 77, 152 left

Chris Dennis – 10, 57 top left, 164

LET THE LAU HITTING SCHOOL PROVIDE YOU WITH:

- Personalized Hitting Instruction
- Video Analysis
- Private Instruction and Appearances

At the Lau Hitting School you'll receive the best hitting instruction available anywhere. And you **will** get results!

NOW AVAILABLE FROM THE LAU HITTING SCHOOL

Training Aides

Designed personally by Charley, these products will enhance your swing and are musts in developing the proper fundamentals.

Instructional Videos

Power With Consistency - Provides live demonstrations of Charley's exclusive drills and includes interviews with many of the game's most prolific hitters.

Secrets of the Swing - This three-part video series will teach you all the secrets of successful hitting. From fundamentals to advances, this video will help you advance, step-by-step, to your full potential.

For More Information on Products or Hitting Instruction Call
305-312-2111
Or Visit Us on the Web at www.lauhitting.com

About the Authors

Charley Lau, Jr.

A sports administration graduate of St. Thomas University, Charley Lau Jr. spent three years as a minor league hitting instructor in the Chicago White Sox organization before returning home to Miami and using South Florida youth leaguers to further validate his hitting development program.

He divides his time between operating Charley Lau's School of Hitting in Hollywood, Florida, and serving as the personal hitting instructor for numerous big-league players. Always well-respected, Charley Jr.'s reputation as a special batting coach grew rapidly after a skinny kid named Alex Rodriguez used his system to not only catapult himself out of the minors, but to also win a major-league batting title.

Charley Jr. has worked with such players as Tony Gwynn, Dante Bichette, and several other high-profile hitters.

Jeffrey Flanagan

Jeffrey Flanagan has worked the last 10 years at the *Kansas City Star* as a columnist, national baseball writer, and a beat writer covering the Kansas City Royals. Prior to that, he worked as the national baseball writer for the *Arizona Republic* in Phoenix. He has also worked at the *Decatur* (Ill.) *Herald and Review,* and the *Portsmouth* (New Hampshire) *Herald.* Flanagan is a graduate of the University of Minnesota with degrees in political science and journalism. He hits and throws right-handed and currently resides in Westwood, Kansas.